Thomas Haupt

Cockatiels

Caring for Them
Feeding Them
Understanding Them

Translated by Celia Bohannon

Photography: Karin Skogstad
Illustrations: Renate Holzner

BARRON'S

CONTENTS

1 What You Need to Know Beforehand

How Cockatiels Live in the Wild 8
Life in the Flock 9
Natural Enemies 10
Offspring in the Flock 10
Appearance in the Wild 13
The Domestication of Cockatiels 14

Considerations Before Acquiring a Cockatiel 18
Factors in Your Decision 18
Male or Female? 20
Distinguishing the Sexes 20
One Bird or a Pair? 22
Children and Cockatiels 24

Apartment Living 26
Landlords and Birds 26
Condominiums 26
Breeding 26

Tips on Buying Cockatiels 28
Where to Buy Cockatiels 28
What a Healthy Cockatiel Looks Like 30

Favorite Color Variants 34

2 Proper Care and Feeding

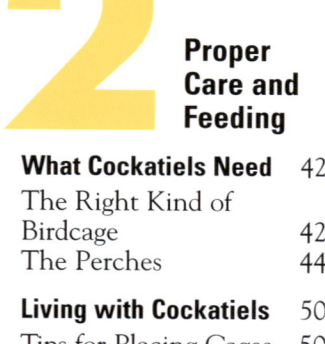

What Cockatiels Need 42
The Right Kind of Birdcage 42
The Perches 44

Living with Cockatiels 50
Tips for Placing Cages 50
Hazards 54
Beware of Houseplants! 55
A Climbing Tree 56

A Varied Diet Is Important 58
Ready-Mixed Birdseed 58
How Much to Feed 61

Proper Hygiene 66
How Do Cockatiels Keep Themselves Clean? 66
Maintenance Schedule 69

Preventive Care and Health Problems 72
Special Features of a Cockatiel's Physique 72
First Signs of Illness 73

Breeding Cockatiels 80

3 Observing and Understanding Cockatiels

What Cockatiels Can Do 90
Behaviors You Should Recognize 90
Speech Sounds 94
What the Crest Indicates 94
Cockatiels Are Clever 94
The Senses 96

Building Trust, Step by Step 98
Building Trust 99
Taming Cockatiels 101
Nighttime Rest 102
First Free Flight 102

Of General Importance

My Cockatiels 118
The Essentials at a Glance 119

Index 120
Useful Addresses and Literature 125
Important Note 127

Fun and Games with Cockatiels 104
Companionship Is Key 104
The Right Toys 108
Speech Lessons 109

Problems and How to Solve Them 112
Fear of Touch 112
Quarrels in the Aviary 115
The Bird Is Too Fat 115
Molting 116
Feather Picking 117

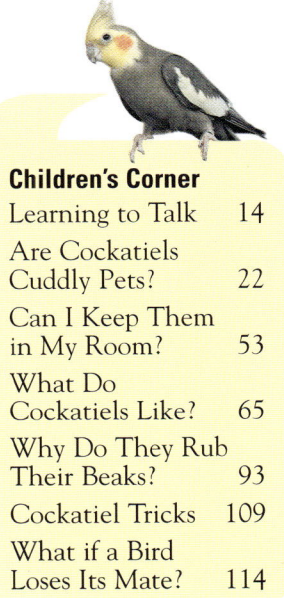

Children's Corner
Learning to Talk 14
Are Cockatiels Cuddly Pets? 22
Can I Keep Them in My Room? 53
What Do Cockatiels Like? 65
Why Do They Rub Their Beaks? 93
Cockatiel Tricks 109
What if a Bird Loses Its Mate? 114

What You Need to Know Beforehand

Cockatiels have been bred in captivity for so long, over 150 years, that it's easy to forget where they originated in the wild. Their natural habitat lies in Australia.

WHAT YOU NEED TO KNOW BEFOREHAND

How Cockatiels Live in the Wild

Cockatiels are found throughout Australia except in the wet coastal regions. Preferring open terrain with wide vistas, they often live near rivers and streams. Cockatiels are also common in agricultural areas, where fields of grain offer abundant food. Their basic diet consists of the seeds of grasses such as spinifex, various seed-bearing weeds, and fruits and berries.

Adjusting to the Climate

Australia's climate is one of wide variations. Temperatures can rise to more than 86°F (30°C) in the daytime and drop to below 32°F (0°C) at night. The cockatiels withstand these severe changes quite well.

In the cold, they fluff up their feathers to capture an insulating layer of air and huddle close together to share their body warmth. To survive the midday heat, they drink copious amounts of water and

A male cockatiel in natural gray with attractive markings.

LIVING IN THE WILD

In flight, the white wing patches are clearly visible.

bathe in the morning dew, in water holes, or in small pools. Dozing in the shade and fanning themselves with outstretched wings also help to regulate their body temperature.

The cockatiels' natural habitat is not one that has a regular rainy season. Rainfall can be quite sporadic. This has an effect on the breeding behavior of individual pairs and of the entire flock.

Life in the Flock

Cockatiels generally live at least in pairs, but usually in small flocks. As many as a thousand birds may gather at watering holes, however, during annual migrations.

In their search for food, water, or a suitable nesting site, cockatiels roam for weeks across the entire country. Luckily, they are excellent fliers and take this extensive search in stride. The birds feed primarily on the ground. They also land in order to drink. While on the ground, they are quite timid and wary, because they are vulnerable to predators and their movement is relatively awkward and helpless.

The individual cockatiel's greatest protection lies in the cohesiveness of the flock. Flying swiftly and in a straight line, the birds emit relatively loud calls to keep in contact with each other. On the ground, by contrast, they are very quiet.

The entire flock stays together during the day's activities. If a few birds

9

WHAT YOU NEED TO KNOW BEFOREHAND

An impressive flock has gathered on this tree.

take off to get a drink of water, all the other cockatiels follow. One exception is in brooding and raising of the young. Here the parents only work together as partners.

Natural Enemies

The chief natural enemies of the cockatiel are birds of prey, which especially target the young, the weak, and the sick. In a flock that stays close together, however, the predator has a very difficult time concentrating on a single victim.

Snakes, although they do not prey on adult birds, can attack the nest, eating the eggs or nestlings that are too young to fly.

Humans, too, number among the cockatiel's enemies. The birds are often hunted unmercifully by farmers, for a flock can do significant damage in a field of grain ready for harvest. Cockatiels also fall victim to motor vehicles, storms, drought, and brushfires.

Offspring in the Flock

Water, food, and nesting possibilities are the most

NATURAL ENEMIES

1 WHAT YOU NEED TO KNOW BEFOREHAND

Basic Information About Cockatiels

Distribution	Throughout Australia, except in wet coastal regions.
Habitat	Grassy plains, arid and semiarid regions, agricultural regions, always with water sources.
Appearance	Natural color is mostly dark gray (see page 14). Many captive-bred variants exist, with different colors and markings and varying size of crests.
Size	About 12.6 in (32 cm) from crown to tip of tail.
Tail length	About 5.9 in (15 cm) long.
Weight	About 3–3.5 oz (80–100 g).
Life expectancy	Up to 15 years, in rare cases longer.
Sexual maturation	At about 15 months.
Breeding time	In native habitat, usually between August and December.
Molting	More pronounced at end of breeding period, but individual feathers fall out from time to time year round.
Number of eggs per clutch	On average 4 to 5 eggs, occasionally more.
Egg-laying intervals	One egg every two days.
Start of brooding	Usually after the second egg.
Length of incubation period	18 to 21 days.
Nestling period	About 33 days.

important factors for successful reproduction in the wild.

If there is a change in the flock's local environment, for example if a drought occurs or fields are harvested, cockatiels will gradually feel the urge to migrate elsewhere. At first only a few birds will be restless, but eventually the entire flock will take off in search of new territory. They may return to an area they have previously

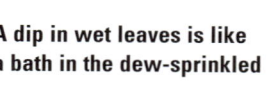

A dip in wet leaves is like a bath in the dew-sprinkled grass.

BREEDING AND RAISING THE YOUNG

TIP

All the cockatiels now sold in pet stores are bred in captivity. Wild birds have not been sold commercially for decades. Therefore, you should not feel guilty about buying cockatiels. The creatures have become accustomed to living in the care of humans.

inhabited, but this happens only by coincidence.

In Australia, cockatiels usually breed between August and December. In rare instances, however, they may breed at any other time of the year.

Cockatiels nest in holes. Suitable holes are found in the branches of older trees or in fallen logs. Because such trees are rare, cockatiels are not particularly territorial about their nesting sites.

Furthermore, the presence of a flock ultimately means safety for the individual fledglings. Other cockatiels are driven away only from the area immediately surrounding the nest opening.

Soon after selecting a nest hole, the female begins to lay eggs. She lays one egg every two days, for a total of two to five eggs, which she and her mate take turns sitting on. After about 19 days, the eggs hatch, about one every two days. The hatchlings, naked and helpless, snuggle close together to stay warm and upright. The mother tends to her brood closely, keeping them warm and fed. At first she feeds them herself, with food her mate brings to the nest entrance.

The larger the nestlings grow, the more the father takes part in feeding them. After about four to five weeks, the young cockatiels scramble to the rim of the nest hole, where they train their wings. Then they venture out onto the branches of the tree, where they are tended to for another two to three weeks. Care of the fledglings is usually the father's job.

The young cockatiels learn about life in the flock, congregate as juvenile groups within the flock, and finally are integrated into the flock as a whole.

Appearance in the Wild

Body: More slender and delicate than the domesticated members of the species.

WHAT YOU NEED TO KNOW BEFOREHAND

Plumage: The birds are gray to grayish black. The crest, brow, and cheeks are yellow.

Both male and female have an orange spot on each cheek that is brighter in the male. The shoulder patches and greater wing coverts are white. The female bears a gray mask with a yellow tint, the male an intense yellow mask. Both have a featherless gray ring around the eyes.

Tail feathers: The upper and middle tail feathers are pale gray, while the underside of the tail is dark gray. In the female, the underside is barred with yellow stripes.

Beak: The beak is gray.

Way of life: Nomadic flocks roam throughout the country in search of food, water, and nesting holes.

The Domestication of Cockatiels

Europeans first voyaged to Australia in the eighteenth century. At the time, the only way to reach Australia was by sea. As seafaring developed, ships increasingly carried goods, products, and animals from Australia to the Old World—to Europe. These included live birds, such as the cockatiels. Cockatiels were first bred in captivity in the mid-1800s in Germany. Because it was not difficult to breed these birds, their numbers multiplied rapidly.

The Latin Name

Scientists classify all living beings in related groups, assigning each to a class,

Learning to Talk

Unfortunately, cockatiels are not as talented in learning speech as the African gray parrot, for instance, or the mynah bird. However, many cockatiels can imitate melodies quite well. Experiment to see whether your pet cockatiels like to do this. It's important that you always play or sing the same tune to your birds. Maybe they will try to imitate the melody. Some cockatiels also learn to repeat words. This takes lots of practice. You should start with very easy words, like "hello" or "bye-bye." Turn to page 109 for more details about the best way to teach your pet cockatiels to talk.

HOW COCKATIELS BECAME DOMESTICATED

A pair of white face pieds. The male tenderly scratches the back of the female's neck.

order, and family. So that scientists anywhere in the world can recognize the organism by its scientific name, Latin and Greek words are used. Each species has a distinctive two-part name. Thus, the scientific name for the cockatiel is *Nymphicus hollandicus Kerr*.

The term *Nymphicus* comes from the Greek word *nymphê* and means "like a beautiful maiden." This identifies the cockatiel as belonging to a genus characterized by a slender "girlish" figure.

The second part, *hollandicus*, is intended to identify the bird's place of origin—New Holland, as Australia was then called. The suffix *Kerr* indicates that a person named Kerr was the first to study and describe the species.

Breeding for Color

Even in the wild, the plumage of individual cockatiels will vary in color. The more brightly colored birds, however, tend to stand out in the crowd of their plain-hued relatives, and unless they are taken captive by humans, or are very lucky, they soon fall victim to predators. Because these

1 WHAT YOU NEED TO KNOW BEFOREHAND

individuals usually do not survive for long, they are unable to reproduce and pass on the genes for bright markings to their offspring.

In captivity, the situation is different. By mating particular birds, the breeder can choose to propagate and establish particular markings and cause others to disappear. Thus, over the course of time, mutations of cockatiels have developed with plumage that differs in color from those of the natural species to varying degrees.

In the wild, cockatiels are gray, possibly with a lighter breast and belly. Some have a hint of light brown. The crest, brow, and cheeks are bright yellow. Both male and female have a large orange cheek patch, which is brighter in the male. The wing and shoulder patches are white. The lower back and upper and middle tail feathers are pale gray. The outer tail feathers and the underside of the tail are dark gray. The featherless ring around the eyes is gray. The beak is gray. The iris is dark brown; the feet are gray. The females have a face mask and crest mixed with gray. The cheek patch is a dull orange; the underside of the tail feathers is yellow, but heavily mottled with dark gray, producing a barred pattern. There are yellowish white flecks on the inner webs of the flight feathers.

Young cockatiels resemble the females in coloration. However, their beak is more pink than gray. They change colors when they are about three months old. Young males often have more yellow feathers in the region of the head.

TIP

Cockatiels have been bred in a wide variety of color markings (see page 34). However, the color of its plumage does not have a major impact on a cockatiel's life, talent, and psyche. With some color mutations, it's simply easier to distinguish between male and female birds.

These two pieds are obviously "in love."

What healthy feathers look like.

BREEDING FOR COLOR MARKINGS

1 WHAT YOU NEED TO KNOW BEFOREHAND

Considerations Before Acquiring a Cockatiel

Cockatiels are good-natured, adaptable, playful pets, easy to breed and relatively undemanding in their daily needs. Nevertheless, there are certain fundamental points to consider before you bring cockatiels into your home.

Factors in Your Decision

1 Cockatiels dwell in flocks and are extremely sociable in nature. Therefore, it's advisable to start with two birds. Even with companionship, however, the birds will need your daily attention as well as the stimulation of variety in their caged existence. Are you prepared to provide your pets with the living conditions they need?

2 The average life span of a cockatiel, given proper care, is 15 years. Can you be responsible for your pet for that long?

3 Cockatiels need a spacious cage or indoor aviary. Both are expensive. Their everyday food is also an expense. If they get sick, you must consult an avian veterinarian. Have you taken these costs into consideration?

4 The birds require food and fresh water each day. Once a week, the cage needs a general cleaning. Do you have the time for these tasks?

5 Picture your cockatiels flying around the room. There's a good chance that they will soil the furnishings (see page 102). Can you live with that?

6 Children (see page 24) may beg for a pair of cockatiels, then lose interest after a while. If this happens, are you prepared to assume responsibility for the birds' care?

7 Do you have a reliable person to care for your cockatiels when you are away on vacation or for another reason?

8 Do you have other household pets (see page 23) that might not get along with cockatiels?

9 Cockatiels warble and chirp, even shriek. Will this bother you or others?

10 Is anyone in your home allergic to feathers (see page 66) or their dust? Does anyone in your family not like birds?

FACTORS IN YOUR DECISION

Two pearled birds. Cockatiels are ideal "starter" birds for novice bird-keepers.

WHAT YOU NEED TO KNOW BEFOREHAND

Male or Female?

If you don't intend to breed your cockatiels, it doesn't much matter whether you choose males or females. Both males and females, if purchased while they're still young, become equally tame.

The cock, as the male is called, has a greater talent for mimicry, however. He has a natural tendency towards posturing and display as he seeks to impress his rivals and court a mate. One of the ways he does this is to imitate the sounds he hears.

Note: Of course, not every cock will learn to repeat words or to whistle back a melody.

Distinguishing the Sexes

It's particularly difficult to tell the difference between males and females when the cockatiels are young, for at this point they still look almost the same.

For older birds, particularly those with natural coloration, the most distinctive differentiating feature is the yellow mask, seen only in males. In young cockatiels, the mask is still quite pale. It brightens when the cock is about eight to nine months old.

The mask, that is, the part of the face that's distinct in color from the rest of the background plumage, can become very bright yellow in males of certain types. The female's face is the same color as the body, though in some mutations it has a light yellowish cast.

The most important distinctive feature in female cockatiels (hens) of almost all variants is the yellow-and-black wavelike stripes

TIP

It's often said that only males will become tame and learn to speak. In fact, however, both cocks and hens are equally likely to become tame. But males, with their innate display behavior, are more likely to try to imitate the voice of their keeper, whom they view as both a role model and a rival.

Dogs and cockatiels should not be left together without supervision.

DISTINGUISHING THE SEXES

A fresh sprig of rose hips delights this cockatiel.

WHAT YOU NEED TO KNOW BEFOREHAND

across the underside of the tail. Also, the edges of the tail feathers are white in females, gray in males.

Note: If you are not sure whether your bird is a male or female, consult an experienced breeder, pet store owner, or avian veterinarian.

One Bird or a Pair?

In the wild, cockatiels live in flocks. They have a very strong need for social interaction and for the physical proximity of a mate. It's basically impossible for a human to satisfy this need for a solitary cockatiel in captivity.

At least two cockatiels must be kept together if the birds' natural needs are to be met. Of course, this also requires that the birds can be sheltered in a cage of appropriate size (see pages 42–44).

Cockatiels kept separately become more attached to their keeper, but they also require much more attention and entertainment. They need stimulating activities and engaging pursuits every day.

A *pair of cockatiels* may mate even if the owner has

Are Cockatiels Cuddly Pets?

You won't make any bird happy by grabbing it and trying to pet it. A cockatiel, too, would feel confined and unable to escape.

However, your pet cockatiel will be delighted to perch on your shoulder. From this vantage it can watch with interest everything you do all day. If it spies something new, the bird will first observe it carefully and then, if possible, explore it thoroughly with its beak. Another enjoyable interaction is to let your cockatiel climb onto your outstretched finger, hold it up before you, and talk softly to it. You can lure almost any bird onto your hand with a stem of Italian millet.

no intention of breeding them. In that case, the hen may lay eggs, but she will brood and hatch them only if a suitable nesting box is available.

Two male or two female birds generally get along just as well as a pair. This is especially

ONE COCKATIEL OR A PAIR?

This pearl pied shows how agile a cockatiel can be.

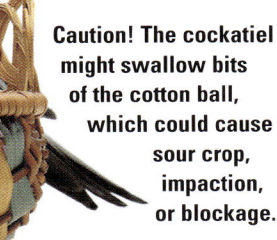

Caution! The cockatiel might swallow bits of the cotton ball, which could cause sour crop, impaction, or blockage.

true if they are placed together at an early age.

In case of doubt, either bird can take on the role of the missing mate. This results in a sort of relationship of convenience, or mock marriage.

If you keep more than two birds, you should take care to ensure a balanced distribution of the sexes. Living in community with others of their kind, the birds will not become as tame as a solitary cockatiel. However, they offer many interesting opportunities for observation, and cockatiels do develop a certain familiarity with their keeper.

Cockatiels and Other Pets

As a rule, cockatiels get along well with other pets.

Dogs, as long as they don't have a strong hunting instinct, will usually not be a problem. However, dogs

WHAT YOU NEED TO KNOW BEFOREHAND

and cockatiels should not be left together without supervision.

Cats are keen predators by nature. Even if the birds are safe in their cage, many cats will try to paw at them between the bars. This disturbs the cockatiels and causes them constant stress.

Small mammals, such as hamsters, guinea pigs, mice, and rabbits get along just fine with cockatiels.

Children and Cockatiels

Birds don't like to be handled, and therefore they are not good playmates for small children. Children want to carry their pets around, hug them tight, and pet them. If they do this with a cockatiel, they might unintentionally be too rough, which could injure the bird's delicate body.

On the other hand, if a child of seven years or older is interested in keeping cockatiels and is carefully taught how to care for birds, a close friendship may develop and endure many years. The child will learn at an early age how to take responsibility for a fellow creature. Daily conversations about the bird—how it's doing, whether it's lively, what it ate—help to sustain the child's interest and give you, the parent, a view of this developing partnership.

Only a child 12 years old or older is capable of taking care of birds independently and handling them properly. Even then, an adult should check now and then to see that all's well in

Options for Vacation Care

1. Leave the birds on their own:
Cockatiels are happiest and safest in their own familiar surroundings. If you will be away for only a day or two, it's all right now and then to leave the birds in their cage with enough food and fresh water. Under no circumstances should they be allowed to fly unsupervised. The risk of injury is much too great. If you must be away for a longer period of time, plan ahead to arrange a suitable alternative.

2. Engage a bird-sitter:
The best choice is a reliable person who can come in and take care of the cockatiels while you are away. Leave a written schedule for feeding and chores, the telephone number and address of your avian veterinarian, a telephone number where you can be reached, and an adequate supply of food.

3. Find a temporary home:
You might be able to find a pet store or an animal boarding facility that will keep your cockatiels. Inquire ahead to reserve space. A friend or relative may also be happy to have your cockatiels visit for a while. However, exposing your birds to others invites disease and could result in tragedy. It is best to keep your birds at home or board them where there are no other birds.

4. Take the cockatiels with you:
This is the least satisfactory option. A new environment and the trials of travel are always stressful for pet birds. Only if your destination is your own vacation home, a short distance away by car, might you take the birds with you in their familiar cage. Never allow the birds to be exposed to drafts, heat, or blazing sun. You can take a practice trip with the cage in your car in advance. If you are going abroad, you must find out about any restrictions on importing birds. Your avian veterinarian may be able to provide this information.

A tame cockatiel enjoys a bird's-eye view of the action. This one prefers to ride shoulder-high.

the birdcage. It's not uncommon for veterinarians to see a starving cockatiel.

Cockatiels, like other birds, hide signs of illness very well. This is an important line of defense, both within and outside of the flock, as even fellow flock birds tend to pick on or attack the sick and the weak. Hence, adult supervision is especially important with pet birds, whose subtle signs of illness may elude young children.

1 WHAT YOU NEED TO KNOW BEFOREHAND

Apartment Living

Landlords and Birds

Landlords are generally cautious about allowing pets in their apartments. Your lease may specifically forbid you having a pet of any type, or it may forbid dogs, cats, or animals exceeding a certain size or weight. Do not assume that your landlord won't mind if you bring in a few animals, even if the animals are just birds. Ask when you rent your apartment, or ask before you buy and bring the cockatiels home. In the United States, breaking one of the rules within a lease agreement is considered breaking the lease, and legal action can follow; at the very least, your stay in the apartment may be uncomfortable and limited. If your landlord does allow pets, a modest damage deposit may be required.

Admittedly, cockatiels aren't likely to cause serious damage to the dwelling; they don't spend any time outdoors, where neighbors might object, and they don't cause odors if the cage is kept properly clean. The only time a problem might arise is if you are keeping a large number of birds for breeding purposes. In that case, the noise might be loud enough to disturb the neighbors. It's always best to be considerate.

Breeding birds are typically louder than pet cockatiels, as they are more territorial and will defend their nest and cage with loud shrieks. Large numbers of breeding birds will only exacerbate this problem and hence are not recommended in apartments.

It is best to keep your pet cockatiels away from dividing walls that separate your apartment from your neighbor's, as, depending on building construction and insulation type, even a single pet bird might be heard by, and possibly disturb, your neighbor.

Condominiums

Although you will own your condominium, every condominium association has specific rules and regulations. Some do not allow pets at all, while others follow certain pet restriction policies, such as allowing dogs under a certain weight and cats that are kept indoors. Frequently pet birds that are kept in cages are not a problem if they are not too noisy; however, it is best to consult the condominium association before you purchase your cockatiel.

Breeding

Breeding cockatiels is a common hobby among pet bird lovers. Cockatiels are among the easiest of psittacine birds to breed and are quite happy to do so in both small, single-pair cages or large multiple-pair flock cages. Hence, large spacious caging is not logistically required for breeding cockatiels, although it is healthier. Ideally, birds should be able to stretch their wings, fly about their cage, and be exposed to fresh air, sunshine, and rain when possible. All psittacine birds do best in outdoor aviaries where weather and space permits.

Cockatiel chicks that are hand-raised make the

best pets. They bond well with their new owners and are more likely to be friendly to others than parent-reared birds. Eggs can be naturally incubated and then babies pulled from the nest and hand-fed after 14 days.

Being the most common and relatively inexpensive pet bird, cockatiels are always easy to sell to pet stores or private owners. Well-cared-for babies will bring in extra income for breeders. Once a client-customer relationship is established with a tidy, well-managed pet store, the cockatiel breeder will be more at ease with selling his or her babies. Sales to private owners are always less stressful, as the breeder can personally screen the new home-to-be indirectly in his or her attempt to place babies in a safe, secure environment.

There are many advantages to banding your birds: identification during and after sale, identification in the event of loss, identification of breeding stock and lineages to prevent inbreeding. However, caution must be taken since bands can become caught, resulting in serious distal limb injuries or worse. Birds can fracture or lose parts of their banded leg and/or foot. In the event of a vicious struggle, even death can ensue if a band is caught. For this reason, banded birds must be kept in neat, tidy cages free of loose, open, or jagged-edged wire, hooks, fasteners, or nails that could snag the banded leg of a curious bird.

Cockatiels should wear leg bands so that they can be identified if they are lost. Also, a closed band identifies a bird as being domestically raised.

Unless you maintain a large number of birds for breeding, you should be able to keep pet cockatiels in a rental apartment.

WHAT YOU NEED TO KNOW BEFOREHAND

Tips on Buying Cockatiels

When purchasing your cockatiels, take your time. Observe the available birds for a good while before you make your selection. This fundamental suggestion, along with the tips given below, may save you from disappointment later on.

Where to Buy Cockatiels

Most pet stores sell cockatiels. Another source of young birds is a reputable breeder.

Conscientious pet store personnel and responsible breeders will exhibit a thorough knowledge of the needs of animals in their care. They will recognize that it is in their best interest to offer only healthy birds for sale.

Wherever you purchase your cockatiels, you should ask for a written receipt. If it should turn out that a cockatiel was sick at the time of purchase, for example, you may be entitled to a refund of part or all of the purchase price. The sales contract should include the following information: date of purchase, leg band number, purchase price, and name and address of both seller and buyer. The sex of the bird should also be recorded if it is an important factor in your choice.

Making the Right Choice

It's important to be personally involved in choosing your cockatiels. Inspect the birds and their living conditions carefully. Here's what to look for:

■ Are the cages where the birds are kept spacious, clean, and bright?
■ Is the supply of food and water adequate and, especially, is it clean?
■ Is there a clean grate over clean paper on the bottom of the cage, and is the paper changed regularly?

Corn on the cob is a healthy snack, and entertaining to boot!

■ How do the birds behave? Do a lot of them seem to be sleeping? Are there many birds with ruffled feathers?
■ Is the cage crowded, or do the birds have at least

TIPS ON BUYING COCKATIELS

In flight, the cockatiel extends its legs to the rear to minimize wind resistance.

enough space to satisfy their need for movement and flight?

■ If the birds have room to fly around, do they do so?

All these observations and questions are important considerations as you make your choice. If the pet store, the breeding facility, the cage conditions, or the birds themselves do not appeal to you for any reason, you should go elsewhere.

Don't buy a cockatiel unless you are serious about caring for it. Otherwise, both you and your bird will be unhappy.

Why the Bird Should Be a Young One

If you do not intend to breed cockatiels, but simply

WHAT YOU NEED TO KNOW BEFOREHAND

want to keep pet birds for company, it's a good idea to select young birds (see table, page 33).

Young cockatiels usually have not had bad experiences with humans and are still naturally inclined to be trusting. *Make an effort* to find a young bird, about six to seven weeks old. At this age, young cockatiels are especially open to new impressions and new friends.

It's generally much easier to connect with a tame and inexperienced young bird. An older flock bird that has spent time flying about an aviary with a flock may even have already started to look for a mate. Such birds are not easy to tame.

Since the fledgling cockatiel has spent its first four weeks in a nesting box and another two weeks still under its parents' care, it is almost completely independent now. In particular, it no longer needs to be fed by its parents; it is able to eat by itself.

What a Healthy Cockatiel Looks Like

When you choose your cockatiels, you should be in a position to judge whether the birds look healthy. *These are signs of good health:*

■ The bird is lively and alert.
■ Healthy birds groom themselves and maintain contact with others of their kind.
■ When sleeping, a healthy cockatiel usually perches on one leg and tucks its head into its wing feathers.
■ The plumage is smooth and lies flat. The bird has fully developed feathers. Even fledglings already have all their feathers by the time they leave the nest box.
■ The eyes are clear.
■ The nostrils are open and not clogged or wet.
■ The feathers around the cloaca (the term for a bird's anus) are clean.
■ The breastbone is well muscled rather than concave.
■ The feet, toes, and nails are completely intact; that is, there are four toes on each foot. Also, the toes should be free of any feces or other deposits. A

TIP

Take plenty of time when purchasing cockatiels. Make your choices carefully. Observe the birds for a while before you decide. Spontaneous purchases often lead to problems later.

If two cockatiels are obviously a pair, don't separate them; buy both birds, or neither (see page 33).

Ah, the good life—the hen devotedly grooms her cock's crest feathers.

TIPS ON BUYING COCKATIELS

1 WHAT YOU NEED TO KNOW BEFOREHAND

missing toe is usually not a handicap, but it may be a reason to reduce the price.

These are signs of a sick cockatiel:

■ Sick birds are apathetic and often sit still in a corner, or perch alone, if at all. Other birds usually avoid or attack them.

■ The feathers are fluffed. Often, individual feathers or clumps of feathers are missing.

■ The eyes or nostrils may be runny or clogged. Also, the eyes are usually half shut, and the bird sleeps a lot.

■ When sleeping, a sick bird frequently stands on both legs.

■ If the bird has diarrhea, the cloaca is smeared with feces.

■ The skin may be reddened if the bird is dehydrated. Ask the seller to blow into the bird's feathers. This will allow you to glimpse the bird's skin.

■ In sick, thin birds, the breast muscles are reduced in mass, and therefore the breastbone protrudes sharply. This is easy to feel.

■ Matted or sticky feet and feathers are a sign that the bird is not grooming itself properly.

Note: Observe the birds for a good long time. Even healthy birds sometimes rest or withdraw from their comrades for a while.

If you detect various signs of illness, however, you should not purchase the sick bird or any others from the same cage, for they may also be sick.

A savory snack attached to a swing rewards agility.

How to Identify a Young Cockatiel (for birds with natural coloration)

	Young Cockatiel	Adult Cockatiel
Eyes	Black beady eyes.	Black beady eyes.
Plumage	The facial mask is not yet colored. Feather colors are duller than in the adult bird.	The mask is fully developed. The feathers shine with rich color.
Beak	Pinkish gray.	Gray.
Crest	Still small.	Fully developed.

How Do You Identify a Cockatiel Pair?

Cockatiels make friends readily with others of their kind. This can occur in a pet store as well. A pair usually involves one male and one female, but friendships also develop between two birds of the same species and sex.

Pairs should never be separated. Instead, make up your mind to purchase both birds. If you are determined to buy only one cockatiel, choose one that clearly hasn't yet found a partner.

You will recognize a pair by the fact that they sit close together on the same perch and stay in physical and vocal contact with each other.

Although many pairs will not become as tame as a solitary bird, they are very happy together and do not suffer as much as a single cockatiel from being left on their own now and then.

True pairs (made up of a male and a female bird) will also be very entertaining in that they typically exhibit courtship behaviors including display, nesting, and vocalizations.

True cockatiel pairs also distinctly exhibit the differences between male and female feather coloration or dimorphism. These differences are best depicted when the birds of different sexes are side by side.

WHAT YOU NEED TO KNOW BEFOREHAND

Favorite Color Variants

Cockatiels come in a wide variety of colors and markings. The most popular variants are shown on the following pages.

■ **Lutino:** These birds have red eyes, slightly yellowish plumage, and orange cheek patches. The feet are light pink; the beak and claws are of whitish horn.

■ **Pied:** The appearance of the pieds is relatively nonuniform. They have white flecks and patches of irregular size all over their body, on otherwise gray feathers.

■ **Cinnamon:** The body plumage on these birds has a delicate cinnamon tinge. All the other feathered areas, like the crest and head, remain the same color as those of wild birds (see page 16). The nestlings have red eyes, adult birds dark.

■ **Pearled (opaline):** These birds have gray feathers edged with yellow on their backs, throats, breasts, and rump. This creates a pattern that almost looks like fish scales. As in all variants, so in the pearled, the young males at first resemble the females. As they grow older, they lose the pearling, and the adult males resemble those in the wild.

There are also specimens with light, almost white, feathers with dark edges. In this coloration, the crest is dark. The edging is maintained in adult females but disappears in the males.

■ **Silver:** These cockatiels have light, delicate silver-gray plumage.

■ **White face:** In the male, the crest looks pure white. The head region of the female is characterized by a light gray with a lighter background.

■ **Albino:** These birds are pure white, with red eyes. Even the beak and claws are light pink to whitish in color.

Note: All of the colors can be combined by interbreeding. Thus, for example, there are cream-colored or light buff cockatiels, and white ones that are actually very light yellow. Other variations include yellow black-eyed cockatiels, cinnamon pied, cinnamon white face, and a great many more.

FAVORITE COLOR VARIANTS

The breeding of cockatiels in captivity has yielded a wide variety of color variants.

1 WHAT YOU NEED TO KNOW BEFOREHAND

Cock with natural coloring. His yellow mask stands out clearly.

A cockatiel pair with natural coloring nibbles on their perch.

A prettily pied female.

At left: A female white-faced pied.

Center photo: A cinnamon-colored female.

FAVORITE COLOR VARIANTS

Albinos have no pigments in their feathers. They are white, with red eyes.

Above right: Yellow lutino.

A pair of cockatiels with natural coloring, female at left, male at right.

This pied cockatiel loves corn on the cob.

WHAT YOU NEED TO KNOW BEFOREHAND

A pearl white-faced female.

Right: A white-faced cockatiel with dark-edged wings.

A pearl pied with much white in the plumage.

A prettily pearled bird with gray background plumage.

FAVORITE COLOR VARIANTS

A white-faced female with otherwise natural coloring.

These two gray-pearled females are close companions.

Portrait of a pied cockatiel.

This pied enjoys a cornflake treat, though too much is not healthy.

Proper Care and Feeding

It's easy to see, from its appearance and behavior, when a cockatiel is thriving—it displays gleaming plumage, clear eyes, boundless curiosity and a keen desire to be right in the middle of the action.

PROPER CARE AND FEEDING

What Cockatiels Need

Before you bring your cockatiels home from the pet store or breeder, you should have everything ready for your new charges.

The Right Kind of Birdcage

For a bird, no cage is ever large enough. Keep this in mind as you shop for a birdcage. Cockatiels in particular are swift and agile fliers. Even if their cage is spacious, they should be let out now and then (see *Free Flight*, page 102).

The shape of the cage should be rectangular. Round cages are not suitable. Birds aren't like helicopters—they rarely fly straight up, but almost always straight ahead. Therefore, the length of the cage is more important than its height. Furthermore, round cages have vertical bars that don't give the birds places to climb.

The minimum dimensions for a cage for one or two cockatiels are about 32 × 24 × 32 in (80 × 60 × 80 cm).

Note: Here's a rule of thumb for cage size: The birds must be able to spread both wings without impediment. Also, they must always be able to perch upright.

The bars of the cage must be horizontal and should be .5 to .75 in (1.5 to 2 cm) apart. Cockatiels like to climb, and they grip the bars with their beak as they maneuver. Without the proper spacing, the bird's beak or claws might become trapped between the bars. The bars should have a dull chrome finish. Plastic coatings are unsuitable; the birds will gnaw on them and swallow the fragments, which could cause digestive problems or worse.

The birdbath should be made of unbreakable hard

> **TIP**
>
> The cage should have a permanent place in your home. Keep in mind that cockatiels don't enjoy hectic surroundings, but also they won't want to be left alone in a little-used room. A spot by an undrafty window is ideal, because the birds can see what's happening outdoors. Be sure the cockatiels are never exposed directly to the hot sun. The room where the cage is located must always be well ventilated, but the birdcage and the birds must be protected against drafts (see page 50).

A cockatiel will relish a few cornflakes as an occasional treat.

CAGE AND AVIARY

bumping their tail feathers against the bars, damaging their plumage (see *Equipment*, pages 44–48).

Aviaries

A spacious indoor aviary or an outdoor aviary with an enclosed shelter would be appropriate especially if you keep several cockatiels or even an assortment of birds of different species. Cockatiels are quite comfortable in such surroundings,

Swift and nimble fliers, cockatiels need to leave their cages often for free flight about the room.

plastic. If it's designed with a drawer, you'll have an easier time cleaning the bottom of the cage (see page 68).

Be sure that the drawer opens and closes smoothly without sticking.

It's very helpful if the cage has two good-sized doors. This facilitates your daily cage maintenance chores and also makes it possible to remove a tame bird from the cage on your hand.

The perches must be installed well away from the ends of the cage so that the birds aren't constantly

where they can follow their natural behavior patterns. Keep in mind, however, that birds in an aviary usually are not quite as readily tamed as birds kept in cages.

Indoor aviaries are best purchased in a pet store. The criteria for selecting an aviary are the same as for selecting a cage. A practical feature for an indoor aviary is a frame on wheels. This allows you to roll the aviary out of the way for housecleaning and even move the birds onto the

43

PROPER CARE AND FEEDING

deck or balcony for fresh air and sunshine on a summer day (see TIP, page 42).

Note: Because aviaries take up so much space, pet stores often don't keep them in stock, but you can place a special order.

An outdoor aviary is an attractive addition to the yard or garden. You might be able to design and build a simple one yourself, or hire a carpenter. Another option is to order a ready-to-assemble structure of the size you need (see photo, page 49).

The Perches

Just as important as the size and location of the cage is the equipment it contains.

Many cages come with perches already included. If these are made of deeply grooved plastic, as is often the case, they will injure the bird's feet, causing a condition called pododermatitis. The same is true of the sandpaper sold in pet stores to wrap the perches, supposedly so that the claws will wear down. In fact, it too damages the soles of the feet.

■ The most suitable perches are sturdy branches of real trees, fastened with slitted ends to the cage bars (see illustration, page 57).

■ Natural branches have the advantage that their irregular surface massages the soles of the cockatiels' feet. Also, the birds gnaw on the bark,

A good feed dish.

Cuttlebone for the beak.

**Above: Mini-birdbath.
Left: Clear plastic box, with vents, for travel.**

OUTFITTING THE CAGE

This well-proportioned cockatiel cage provides enough space for two birds.

adding minerals to their diet, grooming their beaks, and providing entertainment at the same time.

■ Most of the perches should be thick enough so that the birds can't wrap their feet around them, i.e., the birds should be able to wrap their feet 75 percent of the way around the perch. As a result, the claws rub against the branch perch and are worn down. Also provide at least one thinner branch on which the birds can exercise their toes.

■ The number of perches is also important for your birds' well-being. Too many

2 PROPER CARE AND FEEDING

Rose hips add variety to the diet. Both the fruitlets and the leaves are flavorful.

perches restrict their ability to move freely about the cage. It's best to install one perch relatively high, another lower, and a third again high.

Birds will shun a perch that's too low. They prefer a higher vantage point, from which they have a good view of what's happening around them.

Note: For natural perches, choose branches from any unsprayed fruit trees, birches, willows, poplars, nut-bearing trees, and fruit-bearing bushes.

OUTFITTING THE CAGE

Scrub natural branches well and let dry before using.

The branches of coniferous trees aren't toxic, but they often exude a good deal of sap, which can cause a bird's feathers to stick together. Even worse, the bird might take sap into its crop as it gnaws on the branches. In severe cases, this will kill the bird.

Never use branches from trees that have been sprayed or that grow near streets with heavy traffic, where the pollution level is especially high.

A deep, full glass is a safety hazard. The bird might slip head first into the glass and drown.

Feed and Water Dishes

The cage equipment should include at least three dishes: one for water, one for dry bird feed, and one for fruits and seeds (see pages 58–65). For easy cleaning, choose dishes made of metal, hard plastic, or clay, which hang on the bars of the cage. It's important that the dishes are the right size for the birds (see photo, page 44).

Hang the dishes high enough above the perches that the birds can comfortably reach their food and water but won't soil them as they defecate.

Automatic feed dispensers are not recommended. They become clogged, infested, and infected too easily.

Automatic water dispensers are likewise problematic. Too often, the water will sit in the container until it's stale. It's better to give your birds fresh clean water every day.

Cuttlebone

Cuttlebone (also known as a beak whetting stone) completes the essential cage equipment. It is also an excellent source of calcium. The soft side of the cuttlebone should be exposed to the bird.

Cockatiels benefit from the calcium in cuttlebone, since they are finicky eaters and females are prolific layers.

2 PROPER CARE AND FEEDING

Perches made of natural wood provide beneficial exercise for the cockatiels' feet.

Toys and Other Accessories

You will want to be sure that your cockatiels have access to a variety of entertaining activities in their cage.

Pet stores sell suitable toys for cockatiels. Be sure the toys you buy are made of unbreakable materials like stainless steel, leather, or hardwood, which will resist the birds' beaks at least for a while and protect their health. Brightly colored wood on knotted leather cords are fun for curious birds. Wood can be cut into various shapes. Small fresh branches are always the most popular attraction. Cockatiels can spend hours tearing the sturdy twigs apart.

For a bird that's kept alone, however, even the most elaborately outfitted cage and intriguing playthings are no substitute in the long run for attention from and interaction with its keeper. Furthermore, because cockatiels are avid and skillful fliers, they need daily opportunities for free

OUTFITTING THE CAGE

An outdoor aviary enhances the yard or garden while offering the ideal shelter for pet birds.

flight (see page 102). On pages 104 to 109 you will find many other suggestions for keeping your cockatiels lively and cheerful.

Note: Toys made from sisal fibers can entwine and constrict the birds' feet. If the birds swallow bits of fiber, sour crop or impaction can result.

An enclosed birdbath may be fun for some cockatiels, but most birds will ignore it. They much prefer a daily shower, for example from a plant mister filled with warm water and adjusted for a fine spray. The cockatiels will hang from the bars of the cage and enjoy the gentle "rain."

A *nesting box* is needed only if you intend to breed your cockatiels (see Breeding Cockatiels, page 80).

PROPER CARE AND FEEDING

Living with Cockatiels

Gregarious creatures, cockatiels enjoy the company of other cockatiels, but also that of "their" humans. Therefore, you should give careful thought to determining the best location for their cage in your home.

Tips for Placing Cages

1 Wherever you put the cage, it should stay there. Constantly changing the environment, especially during the first few days in their new home, will unsettle the birds.

2 Choose a room frequently used by family members or by the person the cockatiels will relate to most closely. Otherwise, the birds will become lonely and isolated, and they will fail to connect with humans. Pining for company can lead to other problems, such as plucking out their own feathers (see page 117).

3 Place the cage near a window. The sights

Nibble sticks are a tasty treat for birds and keep them entertained as well.

CAGE PLACEMENT

> **TIP**
>
> The birdcage should not be placed directly in front of a stereo system or television playing at high volume. On the other hand, many cockatiels enjoy soft music or sounds from a television. They may chirp or warble in response.

Look! There's another cockatiel in the mirror!

and sounds of the outdoors will fascinate your birds.

Also, your cockatiels can experience the natural rhythm of day and night. Furthermore, if the sun shines through the window, your birds may enjoy a sunbath. It's essential, however, to ensure that they can retreat into a shady area.

4 The cage or aviary should be at your eye level. This gives the birds a good view of their surroundings as well as constant contact with you and your activities. If possible, the cage should also be set against a wall. This increases the cockatiels' sense of security and protects them against drafts.

Note: If the cage is placed too low, the birds feel uneasy. Cockatiels react to danger by taking flight, and their primary natural enemies are birds of prey, which strike from above. If you are working around a cage that is placed very low in the room, the birds have the impression that they are under attack. However, don't raise the cage too high, either; your birds would then remain relatively shy, because they would be unable to participate in the daily life of the household.

5 The cage must be in a well-lighted location where the temperature is comfortable. Avoid a site in the immediate vicinity of a heater. The hot air, rising, dries out the birds' mucous membranes and illness may result.

6 Avoid unnecessary noise; on the other hand, the room should not be dead quiet. Sounds are part of a healthy environment.

7 Nobody should smoke in the room where the birds are kept. Cockatiels' lungs are too sensitive and too delicate to tolerate the harmful substances in tobacco smoke.

Bird-Proofing the Room

Before you release your cockatiels for their first free

2 PROPER CARE AND FEEDING

flight, you must make the room safe for them. Turn off ceiling fans, cover windows, and remove or hide electrical cords.

For instance, many birds have become ensnared in draperies, where they strangle. If the curtains are pulled back from the windows, a cockatiel may crash into the windowpane and break its neck. Cupboards and bookcases that are not set flush against the wall also have cost many a bird its life. If your cockatiel slips into the space between the furniture and the wall, it usually cannot be extricated without injury. Birds have drowned in flower vases and in toilets. The curiosity of cockatiels knows no bounds—they will not hesitate to gnaw on electric cords. If the wires are live, this can end in death. Other hazards, and ways to eliminate them, are listed in the table on page 54.

Note: Never leave your cockatiels unattended when they are loose in a room. Even if you are convinced that the room is entirely bird-proofed, there is always the possibility that the birds will outwit your best intentions.

The Greatest Risk: Escape

Cockatiels can fly at tremendous speeds. If a window is open even slightly while your birds are flying freely about the room, they will escape in an instant. One of my friends tells the story of a cockatiel that seized its opportunity.

This cockatiel's favorite spot is on "his" human's shoulder.

AN ESCAPED COCKATIEL

Can I Keep Them in My Room?

It's better not to keep the birdcage in your bedroom. Birds wake up very early in the morning. Their twittering will awaken you too, especially on mornings when you'd rather sleep in. What's more, you probably don't spend a lot of time in your room during the day, and the cockatiels would be left alone. But cockatiels are sociable birds. They need contact with "their" humans for their own well-being and also if they are to become at all tame. Your cockatiels will be happiest in a room where they can sleep in peace at night but where there's plenty of activity during the day. Cockatiels are naturally curious and enjoy anything new and interesting.

As my friend was leaving the room on the second story of his house, his cockatiel zipped past him in the doorway. Following the air current from the open front door below, the bird flew to freedom. Once outdoors, a bird will swiftly gain altitude, instinctively seeking to orient itself by looking for trees or other landmarks. If it sees no familiar features, it will continue to soar farther and farther into the distance. It's very unlikely that a bird that escapes in this way will return or be recovered.

In warm weather, an escaped cockatiel has a fairly good chance of survival—unless it falls victim to a bird of prey or a cat, is hit by an automobile, or is electrocuted on a power line. To feed itself, the bird can forage for seeds in the grass or fruits and berries on trees and bushes.

In winter weather, an escaped cockatiel might survive for a short while by joining the wild birds and seeking nourishment from birdfeeders.

Fugitive birds are lucky if they are particularly tame, or so hungry that they seek contact with humans. If you see this happening, it's a good idea to try to capture the cockatiel (see TIP, page 55).

Note: To prevent escape, install screens on the windows in the room where your birds are kept. This allows you to open windows for fresh air even when the birds are out of their cage.

2 PROPER CARE AND FEEDING

Hazards

Source of Danger	Danger to Cockatiel	Preventive Measures
Open doors.	Cockatiel perches on door as observation post. Feet are trapped when door is closed.	Always keep an eye on the bird. Don't slam doors.
Clothing scattered on floor.	Cockatiel hides in and under clothes, might be stepped on.	Make it a habit to be careful. Don't leave clothes lying around.
Containers filled with water.	Cockatiel slips or falls into container and drowns.	Cover any containers filled with water.
Poisons such as alcohol, lead pencils, felt-tip pens, ball-point pen cartridges, salt, glue, adhesives, paints, solvents, fertilizers, plastic, cleaning agents, mercury, objects that contain lead or zinc, chocolate.	Poisoning.	Keep all these substances out of reach of cockatiels. Never give your bird alcohol as a joke.
Stove burners, electric irons, open fires, candles.	Cockatiel might burn feet, feathers or flesh.	Keep bird in cage when these hazards are present.
Hot sun, overheated car.	Heatstroke, circulatory collapse.	Provide shade, ventilation.
Heated teflon-coated substances.	Teflon toxicity.	Do not overheat substances coated with teflon.
Electrical appliances.	Burns, electrocution from gnawing on electric cords.	Keep out of reach. Cover cords securely.
Sharp objects, cactuses.	Injury, bleeding.	Keep cactuses away from birds. Never leave sharp objects around.

HOUSEPLANTS

> **TIP**
>
> It's possible to recapture an escaped cockatiel if it has landed, for example, in a tree in your yard. Soak its feathers with a strong stream of water so that it can't fly. You must do this very quickly, however. Another option is to set out an open cage and hope the bird will find its way inside. This works better if there's another cockatiel calling to it from another cage close by.

Also, make it a habit to keep all doors closed.

Beware of Houseplants!

Cockatiels, like all hook-beaked species, love to gnaw on plants. However, they don't know instinctively which are toxic. Therefore, you must take precautions to prevent poisoning.

Poisonous plants include Chinese primrose, nux vomica, dieffenbachia, crown-of-thorns, periwinkle (*Catharanthus*), yew, hyacinth, myrtle (*Vinca*), nightshade, poinsettia, Madagascar palm, narcissus, oleander, spiceberry (*Ardisia*), croton (*Codiaeum variegatum*), desert rose, and asparagus ferns, to name only a few.

Harmful plants include ivy, monstera, flamingo flower, golden trumpet, Chinese evergreen (*Aglaonema*), philodendron, schefflera, and shrubs with resinous branches.

Prickly cactus plants present a serious hazard to birds (see page 54). Accidents are not uncommon, especially with inexperienced and awkward fledglings.

Safe plant materials include fruit-tree branches, nut trees, birches, willows, cat grass, dandelions, and chickweed.

Note: The simplest solution is to keep all houseplants away from birds. If you do purchase plants, inquire in detail whether they are harmful in any way. Offering fresh, non-toxic branches with leaves should lessen the birds' interest in houseplants.

An open door is a favorite perch. Close doors carefully to avoid pinching the bird's feet.

2 PROPER CARE AND FEEDING

A Climbing Tree

While they're flying freely about the room, your birds might nibble on furniture or wallpaper to amuse themselves. The only way to prevent this is to give the cockatiels something more attractive to play with, such as a climbing tree or a free-hanging perch.

Climbing trees and free-hanging perches are sold in pet stores. With a little ingenuity and skill, however, you can build either of these yourself.

Materials for a climbing tree:

■ For the base, use a good-sized planter made of wood, copper, clay, or plastic. If you mount the container on rollers, it will be easy to move around.

■ For the tree itself, find a sapling or stout branch with several branches. The branches will naturally vary in size, providing a good range of exercise for the birds' feet. The cockatiels can also file their beaks and claws against the wood. Good choices include all types of fruit trees (unsprayed), oaks, elders,

You can easily build a climbing tree like this one. Decorate the tree with toys, fresh sprigs, and appealing treats.

A CLIMBING TREE

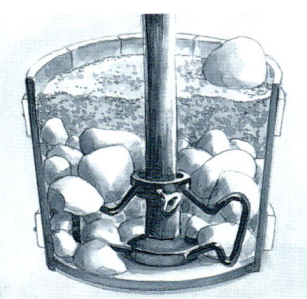

The climbing tree must be absolutely stable.

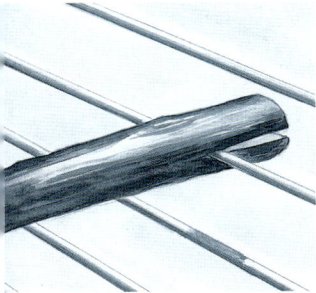

Here's how to fasten natural perches to the bars.

Blow empty seed hulls out of feeding dish.

birches, nut trees, lindens, willows, poplars or chestnuts (see page 44).

After cutting the branches, scrub them well with water and hard soap and let dry.

■ The most important feature of a free-standing perch is its stability. To achieve this, you will need several heavy rocks, a Christmas tree stand, and sand, dirt, or potting soil.

■ The best way to fasten decorations and other items to the tree is with natural-colored hemp.

How to build a climbing tree:

■ Set the trunk or stout branch in the Christmas tree stand and fasten it firmly. Place the stand in the planter, then weight it down with large rocks.

■ Fill the planter with sand, dirt, or potting soil to about 1.9 in (5 cm) below the edge. Cover with a generous layer of bird sand.

■ Trim the horizontal branches so they don't extend beyond the edge of the planter. This increases the odds that any bird droppings will land on the sand in the planter.

■ Decorate the climbing tree appropriately for your cockatiels. To provide more opportunities for climbing, attach additional horizontal branches with hemp so the birds don't hurt themselves on the wire. Swings, ladders, wooden rings, climbing ropes, and little bells add interest and variety to the cockatiels' playground.

Sprigs of parsley, basil, or other herbs can be fastened to the branches with a wooden clothespin. Slices of apples and pears, speared on a nail, invite nibbling. Cockatiels also delight in gnawing on fresh branches, complete with bark.

Cleaning the climbing tree:

The top layer of sand in the planter will need to be replaced from time to time. Scrub soiled branches with hard soap and water.

Note: Place the climbing tree or free-hanging perch far enough from the cockatiels' cage that they are encouraged to fly freely. Never let a cockatiel fly or play outside its cage unsupervised. Climbing tree time is a supervised activity.

PROPER CARE AND FEEDING

A Varied Diet Is Important

Because cockatiels in their native habitat roam widely in search of food, they do not always find foods with the same degree of ripeness. Thus, in Australia the baby birds are generally fed by their parents with half-ripened seeds, usually from various grasses. For the rest of the time, the cockatiels are more likely to eat ripened seeds from grasses, as well as bark, fruit, sometimes small insects, and also grains like wheat, oats, and barley from farmers' fields.

Ready-Mixed Birdseed

Ready-mixed birdseed diets are not the best bird food choice for cockatiels because these birds seek out high-fat foods. Hence, they have a tendency to binge on the fatty seeds, such as sunflower, and are consequently disproportionately plagued by obesity, lipomas, hepatic lipidosis, infertility, atherosclerosis, and general malnutrition, specifically hypovitaminosis A. This is especially true if they are offered only ready-mixed birdseed diets that are notoriously high in fat, low in vitamins A, D, K, B-12, C, and low in calcium, sodium, choline, and the essential amino acid lysine. Further, depending on the seed, riboflavin, niacin, phosphorus, iodine, copper, zinc, manganese, and selenium may also be deficient, as well as the amino acids methionine and tryptophan.

Various formulated (extruded and pelleted) bird diets are now commercially available. Formulated diets are more nutritionally sound and much lower in fat than ready-mixed birdseed diets. When mixed with up to 15% fruits and vegetables for variety, formulated diets still form a balanced meal that may be more visually and intellectually stimulating.

A note of caution: Birds on seed diets need to be carefully converted to formulated diets. Although most conversions are successful, certain smaller species, including cockatiels (as well as budgerigars, finches, and canaries), and some particular individuals may take longer, or may choose never to convert at all. For those birds,

Young birds at the feeding dish. A shared meal becomes a feast.

BIRDSEED

seed mixes with a safflower base, completely devoid of sunflower seeds, and containing small grains and millet are best.

The Quality of Food
Bird food needs to be fresh. Hence, it is best not to purchase seed mix or formulated diets from tubs in pet shops. Food stored in this way is unsafe, as there is no way to be certain of its freshness date. Further, do not purchase large quantities of food for storage at home. Buy enough fresh food for a month to a month and a half. We know that birdseed is edible for about two years after

PROPER CARE AND FEEDING

it is harvested. The majority of formulated foods typically have preservatives. So, purchase only manufactured, packaged seed mix and formulated diets after checking the package freshness dates.

Both fresh seeds and grains will germinate. If you are purchasing ready-mixed seed, you can test for germination to determine freshness for yourself at home.

Spoiled Food

A critical aspect of healthy nutrition for any animal is the freshness of its food. With seed diets this is a particular problem, as high-fat foods, such as sunflower seeds and hemp seeds, turn rancid, spoil easily, and hence loose their nutritive value. The time from harvest to sale can be considerable with seeds and grains, and so, as previously mentioned, checking the package freshness date is especially important with ready-mixed birdseed diets.

Signs that seeds have spoiled are mold, rot, and vermin.

Mold: A whitish gray coating develops, with a pungent odor.

Rot: Sharp, penetrating odor; normal bird feed is almost odorless. Slimy coating on the seeds.

Vermin (feed mites): You should not purchase bird feed that is infested. The signs of a mite infestation are

> **TIP**
>
> **Always store your cockatiels' feed in a dry, well-ventilated place. A linen sack, for example, makes a good storage container. Unsuitable containers include screw-top jars, sealed plastic containers, or even plastic bags. If you are not sure whether the food is still good, it's safer for your cockatiels to discard it.**

Fresh greens from the garden enhance your cockatiels' menu.

Vitamin Therapy for Cockatiels

As previously mentioned, ready-mixed birdseed diets are not nutritionally balanced. They are high in fat, low in vitamins A, D, K, B-12, C, and low in calcium, sodium, choline, and the essential amino acid lysine. Further, depending on the seed, riboflavin, niacin, phosphorus, iodine, copper, zinc, manganese, and selenium may also be deficient, as well as the amino acids methionine and tryptophan. Hence, vitamin and protein therapy is a good idea for cockatiels on ready-mixed birdseed diets. Consult your avian veterinarian concerning which type of commercial vitamins and supplementary proteins (e.g., legumes) are safest for your cockatiel. Some commercial vitamins come in the form of powders or liquids that can be placed on moist food or into the bird's drinking water. Care must be taken when anything is placed into a bird's drinking water. Birds will refrain from drinking, to the point of dehydration and death, if their water is tainted. Vitamins applied to moist foods in "moist food only bowls" are probably safer. Take care, however, as moist food, like fruits and vegetables, can foster bacterial growth, especially *Pseudomonas* and *Clostridium sp.*, which can be fatal. Hence, moist foods should never be left in the cage for more then four hours. Sprouted and soaked seeds are particularly dangerous as they can also foster fungal growth.

Vitamin therapy, however, is a bad idea for birds on commercially formulated diets. These diets are more nutritionally sound and much lower in fat than ready-mixed birdseed. Hence adding vitamins to such rations may be dangerous, leading to toxicities or vitamin overdoses.

clumped seeds and fine cobwebby threads.

How Much to Feed

Birds, particularly the smallest ones, have very rapid metabolisms. They must eat small meals frequently throughout the day, as they can only store scant reserves. Hence, it is important to supply an ample amount of fresh, clean food daily. Do not skimp; birds have voracious appetites for their size. Follow package suggested amounts of food for cockatiels and do not hesitate to consult with your avian veterinarian if you have any questions.

When you offer fresh food (and water) to your cockatiel, you should discard all the old food, and clean the bowl with hot water and soap. Fresh seed or formulated commercial bird food must be offered daily. Do not leave any old food in the bowl. This is a very poor unhygienic practice that fosters the development of rancid seed, bacteria, and fungus.

Fruits and vegetables should not be left in the cage, in their specific moist

2 PROPER CARE AND FEEDING

Their gleaming plumage testifies that these cockatiels are fed a healthy and varied diet.

food bowl, for more than four hours, as these soft, moist foods spoil more easily, fostering extensive bacterial and fungal growth.

Fruit, Vegetables, Greens

In the wild, cockatiels never refuse any fruit and vegetables their foraging may yield. They should also have this food source in captivity, for fruit and vegetables contain many essential vitamins and trace elements.

Birds will enjoy whatever bounty is in season.

Fruits and vegetables include, for example, radishes, carrots, apples, cucumbers, kiwi, strawberries, cherries, plums, peppers, red beets, eggplant, celery, peas, tangerines, grapes, peaches, pineapple, raspberries, blackberries, melons, figs, mangoes, and citrus fruits.

Caution is also advisable in the case of leaf lettuce.

FRUIT, VEGETABLES, GREENS

Because of its high water content, it also stores many harmful substances, such as pesticides. This can be harmful to your cockatiels' health. Lettuce from your own garden can be given in small quantities with no worry.

Greens from the garden and the wild add variety to your birds' diet. Examples are basil, parsley, chervil, meadow grass (*Poa annua*), hairy crabgrass (*Digitaria sanguinalis*), vetch, daisies, dandelions, sorrel, shepherd's purse, and watercress.

Note: Be sure that you've picked the right plant. Ask at your local greenhouse or florist.

Gather wild plants only at sites that have not been sprayed and are not too close to a heavily traveled street. Pollutants from the exhaust of motor vehicles are extremely harmful to your birds' health.

How to Prepare Fruit, Vegetables, and Greens

■ Greens, vegetables, and fruit must be carefully washed and patted dry.

■ If you're not sure that fruit and vegetables have not been sprayed, you must peel them. To avoid an accumulation of toxic substances, don't feed too much of one type. As a basic rule, offer as wide a variety of foods as possible.

■ Feed fruit, vegetables, and greens only at room temperature. Food that is too cold can cause diarrhea and other problems.

■ Be sure the individual pieces of fruit and vegetables aren't too large. The bird must be able to move them around and pick them up. On the other hand, pieces that are too small soon lose their firm texture, becoming mushy and unappetizing.

■ Fruit and vegetables can be offered in a separate

Fresh fruit, like this apple, is rich in vitamins.

PROPER CARE AND FEEDING

dish. The regular bird feed should also be available at all times in a separate bowl.
■ If your cockatiels don't like a particular fruit or vegetable, continue to offer it now and then anyway. Often they will try it eventually.
■ Try tying greens into a bundle and fastening it to the bars of the cage with a wooden clothespin, or offering chopped greens and fruit. Many cockatiels also enjoy "splashing" in dewy-fresh greens or leaves in a dish on the floor of their cage (see page 68).

Other Additions to the Diet

Italian millet is a tasty treat for cockatiels, though it is highly perishable. Especially for pairs who are breeding or raising their young, for fledglings, and for birds who are sick, Italian millet is an important dietary supplement.

Here too, however, the rule applies: Give only in moderation. A healthy bird needs at most a spike about 1.9 in (5 cm) long each day.

Long sticks or rods are made of seeds held together with honey. Although they entertain cockatiels for a short time, they are extremely high in calories. Fresh branches are just as much fun to chew on, but without the calories.

The Right Liquids

Fresh, clean water is essential for your cockatiels. If your bird will not drink fresh, clean water, take it to see an avian veterinarian; it may be in need of medical attention.

Vitamins

Because you can't be sure that your sedentary bird will get the vitamins it needs from fruits and vegetables, you should add vitamins to its moist food once or twice a week.

Note: This is not needed if your bird is on a commercial pelleted diet. In fact, it can be detrimental, and result in vitamin overdose.

It's best to obtain a multivitamin preparation from your avian veterinarian.

A whole honey stick for one bird is too much of a good thing.

VITAMINS AND MINERALS

What Do Cockatiels Like?

If you want your pet cockatiels to stay healthy, you must give them a variety of foods. Ready-mixed birdseed or commerical pelleted diets are not enough. They also need greens, fruit, and vegetables. You can collect fresh treats for your birds outdoors. In a meadow that hasn't been sprayed with pesticides, you'll find dandelions and stalks of grasses with seeds still on them. Your cockatiels will surely relish these snacks. Before you give your birds the fresh greens, wash them thoroughly under running water and spread them on a paper towel to dry.

Follow the dosage directions exactly, because an overdose can be harmful.

Minerals and Trace Elements

Cockatiels need minerals and trace elements to build bones and feathers and to grow; females also need them to form eggs.

In the wild, birds ingest soil that contains minerals. Cuttlebone, calcium blocks (from a pet store), or ground hen's eggshells can also serve the purpose. Commercial mineral supplements are also available, as powders that are mixed with the food.

Cockatiels and "People Food"

Many of the snacks your cockatiel might seem to enjoy really are not good for its health. Take note:

Harmful foods: Chips, pretzels, and leftovers from your meals contain too much salt and spices. Candy and cookies contain too much fat, sugar, and coloring agents. Alcohol, chocolate, coffee, and avocados are also dangerous and can kill your bird.

Snacks your bird can share: Fruit juices (unsweetened), dried bread, whole-grain crackers, zwieback, cooked potatoes (cooled), cooked noodles, rice, pasta, lean meat, yogurt, nonfat cottage cheese, mild cheese in small quantities, granola (especially a whole-grain product), and all vegetables and fruits, except avocados, which can kill your bird.

2 PROPER CARE AND FEEDING

Proper Hygiene

New food, like this apple, is first examined thoroughly.

Cleanliness in the cage is as important as hygiene when handling your cockatiels. This prevents illness in your birds, and also keeps you from getting sick. On the other hand, excessive cleaning or constant disinfecting of the cage and equipment will do more harm than good. A cockatiel's immune system is weakened if it is never exposed to germs.

How Do Cockatiels Keep Themselves Clean?

Like most birds, cockatiels are very clean creatures.

Several times a day, a cockatiel spends a long time preening itself. It tidies, cleans, and arranges each little feather, drawing it through its beak to remove dust and other dirt. At the same time, it smoothes the feathers down.

Then it coats each feather with a fatty secretion stored in a special skin gland called the preen

PROPER HYGIENE

TIP

Observe how flexible your bird is as it preens itself. It can turn its head 180 degrees, effortlessly reaching even to its lower underbody.

Preening, side by side. In the bird on the right, it's easy to see how each individual feather is drawn through the beak.

gland. The preen fluid keeps the feathers waterproof, so that a cockatiel can fly even in the rain. The preen fluid also prevents water from penetrating to the skin and protects the bird against freezing.

The preen gland is located on the rump, near the base of the tail. The cockatiel uses its beak to spread this gland's secretions on the feathers. Only the head feathers are rubbed directly on the gland itself.

A cockatiel cleans its beak by rubbing it against a branch or a piece of cuttlebone. This causes dirt to fall off and keeps the edges of the beak trim.

Many Cockatiels Enjoy a Bath

A cockatiel's daily hygiene should also include a bath. For most, the favorite method is a "rain shower." You'll see how they spread their wings wide so the sought-after water reaches every part of the body and not a drop is wasted.

Another trick is to hang, head down, from the top of the cage or aviary and try to catch each droplet.

Be aware that your cockatiels need to bathe like this as often as you can manage it. This is especially true in winter, because household heating systems make the air much too dry for cockatiels.

2 PROPER CARE AND FEEDING

Bathing enhances your birds' well-being, entertains them, and encourages them to preen themselves.

Keep in mind, however, that the daily shower should be given in the morning, or at least during the day, so that the cockatiels have time to dry their feathers. Never leave a bird with wet feathers in a dark room at night. It could catch a cold, or worse.

If you aren't able to indulge your birds with natural rain (in warm weather only, of course), you can create your own rain shower with an ordinary watering can. Be sure the watering can is free of any chemicals or residues.

Fill the can with warm water. Adjust the nozzle to the finest spray, so the resulting mist is soft and comfortable.

If your birds also accept a birdbath—which can be either a wide, shallow clay dish or a commercial birdbath made especially for cockatiels—then they can bathe any time they like.

Note: Some authors recommend offering the birds a shallow dish filled with moistened leaves. The cockatiels can "splash" among the leaves to their hearts' content. The idea is that this replicates the situation in the wild, as cockatiels in search of food flit through tall grass and low branches, dampening their feathers in the early morning dew.

However, the leaves you offer your pet cockatiels must be from unsprayed trees and should not be left for too long in the cage, as they might become moldy or rotten.

Cockatiel Care Made Easy

Both humans and animals feel better in a clean environment than in a dirty one. In captivity, cockatiels

Snack and exercise in one: The cockatiel bends low to reach the tempting millet.

MAINTENANCE SCHEDULE

Maintenance Schedule

Every Day	**Once or Twice a Week**	**Once a Month**	**Every 3 to 6 Months**
• Empty all feed and water dishes, wash in hot water, dry, refill. Remove wilted greens and twigs. Leave millet in cage until it's all gone if clean or dry. • Scrub perches, branches, and cage bars with a stiff brush to remove droppings. Wipe with damp cloth. • Remove droppings and food remnants from grate. Change paper under grate. • Clean birdbath; fill with fresh water. • Observe birds. Are they lively and alert? • Check to be sure all food residues are removed. • For breeding pairs: Is there enough nesting material? Are there any eggs yet? • Clean area around cage.	• Clean cage and equipment (bowls, feed and water dispensers, perches, branches, birdbath) thoroughly with hot water and neutral soap. • Check cuttlebone. • Fasten a fresh stalk of millet in the cage. • Clean out base of cage and wash with hot water. In aviary, remove soiled dirt bedding, rake natural soil, wash stones, rinse branches with running water.	• Remove and replace perches made of natural branches. • If possible, wash down cage in tub with hot water and scrub thoroughly with brush. • Inspect cage or aviary for damage. • Inspect cage or aviary for mites. • If necessary, trim the birds' claws (see page 75). Inspect birds for parasites (see page 74). • Scrub climbing tree thoroughly; wipe down with damp cloth. Remove and replace top layer of sand.	• If birds are kept in outdoor aviary, have feces inspected for parasites (see page 74). • In outdoor aviary, dig up soil to the depth of a spade. Turn over the soil, or replace the top layer entirely. **Note:** All instructions will vary depending on the size of the cage and the number of birds.

PROPER CARE AND FEEDING

depend on their keepers to do what's needed to ensure that the cage and equipment are clean.

Cockatiels make relatively little mess in their cage. A thorough weekly cleaning of the cage, including the base, with hot water and neutral soap will suffice. The cage paper under the grate, however, should be changed daily.

Scrub the perches with a stiff brush to remove all bird droppings. Then wipe the perches down with a damp cloth.

Follow the same procedure for the climbing tree (see page 56). Use a putty knife to scrape droppings from the planter.

Feathers and feather dust can be cleaned up easily with a vacuum cleaner. Use a damp cloth to clean any droppings from furniture in the room. Droppings on the carpet might be more problematic.

If the droppings are dry and firm, pick them up carefully with a paper towel. If the droppings are not dry, use several damp paper towels, warm water, and soap to clean the droppings up

Top photo: The tail feathers are thoroughly cleaned.
Bottom: The flight feathers get special attention.

CLEANING CHORES

The cockatiel brings its foot up under its wing to scratch its face. This is also part of the daily grooming.

immediately. Since cockatiels eat very little animal protein, their excrement has very little odor. Do not let the droppings dry, as they should be cleaned up as soon as possible. The same is true for droppings on soiled clothing; wash them off as soon as possible.

Psittacine bird feces normally has large amounts of gram-positive bacteria, along with a very small amount (1–15%) of gram-negative bacteria. In the event of illness, changes may be seen in the amount of gram-negative bacteria in the feces; typically it will go up. Secondary or primary enteric yeast infections are also possible. Other diseases such as chlamydia are also transmissible through the feces. If your bird is diagnosed with chlamydia by your avian veterinarian, you should contact your physician, as it is a zoonotic (transmissible to humans) disease.

In general, normal, basic hygienic procedures, such as keeping the cage clean and washing hands regularly, are typically sufficient.

PROPER CARE AND FEEDING

Preventive Care and Health Problems

The best way to keep your cockatiels healthy is to give them the right living conditions and proper care. Be sure each cockatiel has at least one other cockatiel to keep it company. Feed the birds a variety of nutritious foods, keep the cage clean, and provide plenty of exercise and other activities. But if a bird does become sick, it's important to respond right away. Don't hesitate to take the sick cockatiel to your avian veterinarian immediately.

Special Features of a Cockatiel's Physique

Most parrotlike species are native to rain forests, where food is abundant. As a result, they do not need to store reserves of fat. Furthermore, by their very nature all birds that fly must be as light as possible, and therefore they have no excess fat storage mechanisms.

On the other hand, fat supplies energy to the body.

Healthy birds enjoy gymnastics on a swing like this one.

SIGNS OF ILLNESS

The cockatiel casts a wary eye at his reflection, thinking it's another cock.

Especially in emergencies, or when it's impossible to get energy from eating, the body normally resorts to digesting its own fat. For a bird, however, this is ordinarily impossible. Furthermore, a bird's normal metabolism is already quite high. For example, its normal body temperature is 108°F (42°C). These circumstances demand a constant supply of energy in the form of food.

A *sick bird* will often stop eating, and its scant reserves are consumed almost immediately. Therefore, you must take a cockatiel to the veterinarian as soon as you detect the first signs of illness.

First Signs of Illness

Even if you monitor your birds carefully, it's not easy to identify early signs of illness. For example, if a bird sits in its cage with its feathers fluffed up, you won't notice right away that it might have lost some weight. Nevertheless, you should make it a daily habit to give your attention to certain specific points: Are the feces normal? Is the bird eating and drinking? Is it sleeping more than usual? Is it spending most of its time perched in one spot with its feathers fluffed up?

First aid: The best thing for a sick bird is warmth. As an immediate measure, offer your bird a dose of infrared light. Cover one half of the cage with a cloth and shine the light on the other half. This allows the bird to decide whether to seek warmth or shade. Test with your hand to be sure the temperature isn't too hot in the bird's vicinity (see illustration, page 78).

Injuries

Whenever several birds are kept together, whether in an outdoor aviary or indoors, injuries are common.

The usual culprits are cats and trauma, but other causes include nesting-box disputes, pecking-order scuffles, and carelessness during free flight.

73

PROPER CARE AND FEEDING

Signs: Blood on the feathers and/or on the perches; broken bones.

Treatment: All wounds need attention. Use pressure to stop minor bleeding, then disinfect with betadine. For severe bleeding, apply gentle pressure and take the bird to the veterinarian at once. A bird with broken bones or other serious trauma also needs veterinary attention.

Parasites

The chief parasites are red bird mites, feather mites, and burrowing mites (*Knemidokoptes pilae*). Cockatiels usually become infested through contact with other birds.

Signs of infestation are normally severe agitation, obsessive grooming, inability to rest or sleep, and sudden startling.

Red bird mites hide during the day in wooden parts of the cage and attack the bird at night to suck blood from its skin. If you hang a white cloth over the cage at night, you will find the mites attached to the cloth in the morning.

Ask your veterinarian for an effective miticide/acaricide. All the wooden parts of the cage must be removed, scrubbed thoroughly, and disinfected.

Feather mites are visible on the feathers with the naked eye. Treatment is the same as for red bird mites.

Burrowing mites cause the dreaded problem called scaly face. These mites live in the unfeathered areas of the skin and in the bird's hornlike parts. They burrow under the skin, causing swelling. If you suspect knemidokoptes, take the bird to a veterinarian.

Tumors

Fatty tumors (or benign lipomas) are the most common tumor in birds, especially those on seed diets. Further, they are more common in older birds. Fibrosarcomas (or malignant tumors) are the second most common tumor in birds. These are most often found in the long bones of cockatiels.

Tumors are always a problem if they are malig-

> **TIP**
>
> It's essential to know your birds well, for only then will you be able to notice changes early. If the symptoms are alarming, take the cockatiel to the veterinarian immediately.

THE MOST COMMON DISEASES

A balanced diet of healthy foods helps prevent illness.

nant. Benign tumors are a problem if they cause local ulcerations or grow so large as to incapacitate the bird. In the early stages, the veterinarian can remove most tumors surgically. Fatty tumors tend to recur.

Feather cysts form when the feather shaft growing inside the feather follicle does not break through the skin, but instead curls over, continuing to grow beneath the skin. In this case, too, a surgical procedure can remedy the situation. If the follicle is successfully removed, the cysts may not recur.

Note: These cysts are not to be confused with an obstructed preen gland, the secretory gland located at the base of the tail. This obstruction must be relieved by a veterinarian.

A *tear in the air sac* makes the bird's skin look as if it has been inflated like a balloon. This is not a growth, but rather a hole in the air sac. A stent in the skin, or repeated expression of the trapped air will keep the bird comfortable while the air sac lesion heals and/or is compensated for by the bird's respiratory system.

Excessive Growth of Beak or Claws

You may notice that your cockatiel gets its claws caught in the curtains, for example, or has trouble eating because its beak is too long.

Possible causes: Age-related changes in metabolism, improper diet, too little material to gnaw on.

Treatment: The claws or beak need to be trimmed, but this must be done by a veterinarian. Blood vessels in the claws can be injured

PROPER CARE AND FEEDING

during trimming. As a preventive measure, be sure to provide a cuttlebone and branches that will promote proper wearing down of the beak and claws.

Constipation

If a cockatiel strains to defecate but its effort is unproductive, it is probably constipated.

Possible causes: Improper diet, ingestion of foreign bodies, tumors, and many other factors. Egg binding in a female cockatiel can also lead to constipation. A veterinarian must make the diagnosis.

Treatment: Only by the veterinarian. If the bird is male and tame, the lower belly can be massaged to stimulate intestinal activity. Infrared light can also help (see illustration, page 78) to keep the bird warm.

Diarrhea

There are three parts to a bird's droppings. The clear liquid portion is the urine. The white, solid portion is the urates and the green solid portion is the feces. The three are mixed in the cloaca, a saclike organ located before the vent, or anus, where the bird's droppings exit its body. If the green portion is runny, the bird has diarrhea. On the other hand, if the white part loses its consistency, or becomes discolored, the bird might have kidney problems.

Possible causes: If the cockatiel seems lively, this may be a harmless nuisance, perhaps caused by excitement or by eating fruit. However, if the bird excretes runny droppings all day long, if it appears dull and lethargic, if the feathers around the cloaca are quite soiled, and if the droppings are even brownish or mixed with blood, these are extremely alarming symptoms whose cause must be determined by a veterinarian.

Treatment: Because a bird with diarrhea loses a great deal of liquid very quickly, you should take the cockatiel to the veterinarian without delay.

As first-aid measures, place the bird in a separate cage to avoid infecting its companions. Radiation with infrared light will do

> **TIP**
>
> A responsible bird owner will be prepared for emergencies, such as an injury. Assemble a small first-aid kit for your cockatiels. Include the telephone number of the veterinarian, gauze pads to stop the bleeding, betadine, Neocalglucon, a small pair of scissors, tweezers, tongs, a magnifying glass, and gauze bandages.

After eating, it's time for a good long stretch.

THE MOST COMMON DISEASES

PROPER CARE AND FEEDING

the patient good (see page 73). Water with a little dextrose supplies a little energy. Clean the cockatiel's soiled bottom with lukewarm water.

Sour Crop or Crop Stasis

If your cockatiel has a slow crop, regurgitates, and gags continuously, it is probably suffering from a condition known as sour crop or crop stasis.

Possible causes: Fungi, bacteria, foreign bodies, spoiled food, parasites, or viruses.

Treatment: Only by a veterinarian. Pressure around the crop may cause further regurgitation, so handle the bird very carefully on the way into the veterinarian.

Concussion

Signs of concussion, CNS trauma, include holding the head crooked, staggering, trembling, falling unconscious from the perch, convulsions, tremors, and paralysis.

Possible causes: Head trauma during flight.

Treatment: Place the cockatiel in a small dark

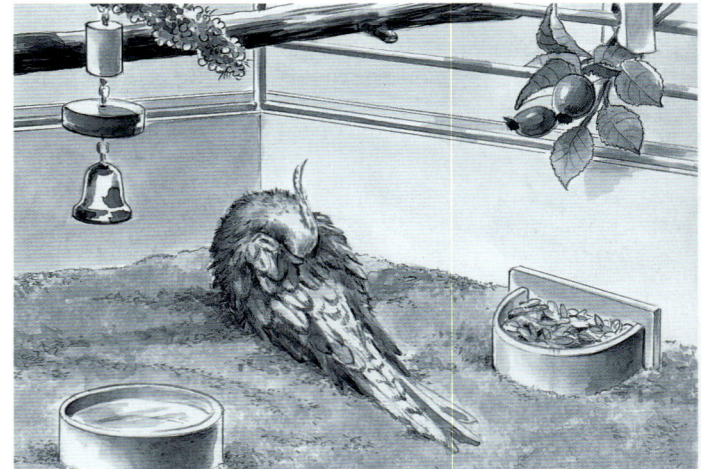

A sick cockatiel sits fluffed up in the corner of the cage, often tucking its head into the feathers on its back.

Warmth helps the patient feel better. An infrared lamp makes a good heat source.

THE MOST COMMON DISEASES

It's easier to administer liquid medications if you wrap the bird in a small towel.

box and call the veterinarian immediately.

Respiratory Tract Disorders

The symptoms range from respiratory distress, noisy breathing, and shortness of breath to pneumonia.

Possible causes: Drafts, smoke, dry and dusty air, bacteria, fungus, parasitic, or other infectious organisms. A veterinarian must make the diagnosis.

Note: If dry air is the problem, a humidifier, an aquarium, or an indoor fountain will help.

Chlamydiosis (psittacosis, parrot fever, or ornithosis) can make both birds and humans very sick. This OIP (obligate intracellular parasite) infection is characterized by sniffling, nasal discharge, apathetic behavior, conjunctivitis, fever, and pneumonia. In humans, signs also include severe flu symptoms, accompanied by a high fever.

This disease, which must be reported to health authorities in certain states, is treatable in both humans and birds.

Note: Because a cockatiel can become infected only by contact with other birds, the risk of contracting psittacosis is low for a bird that is kept indoors and alone.

Taking the Cockatiel to the Veterinarian

Especially in an emergency, you should call ahead to be sure the veterinarian is available. If not, you will generally be given the name of a colleague who can see the bird. Otherwise, you might lose valuable time.

Transport the sick bird in its accustomed cage if small enough, or use a small, dark box lined with a face cloth. This allows the veterinarian to examine the bird's droppings as well. Be sure to cover the cage with a cloth or place it in a suitable cardboard box to prevent drafts.

If you keep your birds in a large indoor aviary, place the sick bird in a carrying box (see photo, page 44).

Be sure to ask your veterinarian how to give medication, apply ointments, and insert eyedrops.

79

PROPER CARE AND FEEDING

Breeding Cockatiels

Cockatiels breed and have offspring without difficulty in captivity as in the wild.

Essentials for Breeding

If you have a harmonious pair, cockatiels can be bred in almost any cage. The reason is that they can't be choosy in their native habitat either, for nesting sites there are few and far between.

A *nesting box* in the cage is all it takes to put a pair in the mood to breed. It's important that the nesting box be of adequate size.

You can choose between a horizontal nesting box and a vertical one—the cockatiels will accept either. The vertical box should have a square base measuring 12 × 12 in (30 × 30 cm) and side walls 14–16 in (35–40 cm) high. For either nesting box, the entry hole must have a diameter of 3–3.5 in (8–10 cm). A vertical nesting box needs something inside to help the birds get in and out. This can be a piece of wire mesh or a wooden ladder.

The horizontal nesting box should have a rectangular base measuring 12 × 16 in (30 × 40 cm) and side walls 10 in (25 cm) high.

For either box, the base should be a board at least 1.5 in (3.5 cm) thick; the walls may be thinner. Also popular with cockatiels are nesting boxes made of slab lumber, that is, boards with the bark still on them. These look like natural tree trunks (see TIP, page 81). It's important for any nesting box to have a removable or hinged lid so that you can look inside. This also makes cleaning easier. Choose only a nesting box made of untreated softwood.

As nesting material, cockatiels in the wild just use bits of wood that they gnaw from the interior wood of their nesting holes, or other material that was already in the hole. Therefore,

A cock performs his courtship display for the reflection in the copper coaster.

COURTSHIP AND MATING

> **TIP**
>
> The most natural nesting site is a hollow tree trunk with an inner diameter of appropriate size. This offers two advantages: Its interior provides a better microclimate, and its rough inner surface makes it easier for the birds to climb in and out.

you can simply line the bottom of the nesting box with shavings. Pine or ash are safest.

Like the box, the nesting material should consist only of untreated softwood.

Note: Often, a hen will remove the shavings from the box. In that case, it's a good idea to make a hollow in the floor of the nesting box so the eggs don't roll away. The hen must be able to gather all the eggs underneath her body to incubate them evenly.

Courtship and Pairing

Cockatiels are remarkably adjustable birds. They can be kept in a flock, in pairs, and even in company with birds of other species. Under any of these circumstances, they will feel the urge to breed,

He seems to think it's another cockatiel.

as long as they have the right partner and the appropriate environmental conditions (such as a nesting box and a varied diet). It's especially charming to watch two birds choose each other from a flock to mate for life.

A *pair* is easy to recognize by their mutual attention and affection. Even if you have only two cockatiels, if they like each other you will be able to watch the whole repertoire of avian courtship behavior. The first sign of mutual attraction is that the birds sit very close together.

This cuddling develops into affectionate nuzzling. Soon it's clear that they have formed a couple. From now on, they do almost everything together. If one eats, the other eats too. If the cock grooms his feathers, the hen grooms hers. The next

81

PROPER CARE AND FEEDING

step is a flurry of caresses from the male. Devotedly, he scratches the hen's head and gives her little kisses with his beak. Finally, he offers his "lady love" the courting song, a melodic and rhythmical warble.

The courting song is intended to attract the female more closely. Then the cock spreads his feathers and runs back and forth along the perch, tapping with his beak and perhaps raising his crest erect. This courtship dance is also intended to impress the hen. She finds it charming when he prances in front of her, spreading his wings to flash his white shoulder patches. Bending and bowing forward, he fans his tail feathers wide. If space permits, the cock will take to the air to show off his flying skills in acrobatic tricks that can be spectacular to watch.

Note: Disputes arise only when a bird attempts to court another that has already chosen a partner, or when two pairs compete for the same nest box. Such scuffles usually end without bloodshed. If you keep several cockatiels, you should try to have a balance of males and females, and provide several identical nest boxes for them to choose from.

Pairing

If the hen is receptive to the cock's advances, she will lie flat on the perch with her tail turned sideways.

This signals that she is willing for him to tread (copulate with) her. Now the male mounts onto her back, crossing his tail feathers beneath hers in such a way

Bottom left: The developmental stages of a cockatiel. This is an adult male with natural coloring.

Bottom center: A fledgling, about three weeks old. Its feathers are almost completely developed.

Bottom right: A hatchling, just a few days old.

The cock tenderly nuzzles his hen. Such head scratching promotes bonding.

that their cloacal vents meet. This allows his sperm to enter and reach her oviduct, where they fertilize the maturing eggs.

The mating act can last for several minutes and is repeated several times, with both birds cooing softly.

When they have finished pairing, the two will sit close together and groom their feathers back into place.

Egg-laying and brooding: The cock slips in and out of the nest box, enticing his mate to enter. Soon the hen begins to spend more and more time within the box, gnawing at the inner walls.

To prepare herself for laying the eggs, she digs at the shavings to form a small hollow. Meanwhile, the cock stands watch outside the nest box.

PROPER CARE AND FEEDING

Laying the Eggs

A hen will generally lay four to six eggs, at intervals of about two days.

The first egg appears about one week after the pairing. Brooding usually begins after the second egg is laid. The two birds take turns brooding their eggs.

If a cock is negligent about doing his share, the hen may not have the patience to do the job all by herself. If she leaves the eggs uncovered for too long, they will cool off and the embryos will die. This mishap can occur with an overeager as well as with an inexperienced pair.

The mating ritual of cockatiels does not include the cock feeding the hen. She flies off to feed herself, while her mate takes his turn brooding the eggs.

It may happen now and then that both birds are away from the clutch, eating or preening. If their absence is brief, you needn't worry; the eggs should stay warm.

If the eggs are fertilized, the chicks will hatch after 18 to 21 days, in the order the eggs were laid. If the birds began to brood the eggs only after the second or third was laid, several hatchlings may appear on one day. The chicks born later are smaller than their siblings for a time, but their parents take just as good care of them. While the nestlings are very small, it's important not to disturb the birds simply out of curiosity. However, it's all right to check now and then to be sure all is well, and to weigh them. All weights should be recorded and evaluated with respect to the birds' age.

Note: A female cockatiel that is kept alone may occasionally lay an egg. Don't remove

TIP

You can tell whether an egg is fertilized by "candling" it after about four to six days. Hold the egg up to a strong light. Fertilized eggs show a small red spot (the embryo) with blood vessels radiating from it. Unfertilized eggs are clear. (See illustration, page 87.)

For a bird kept alone, a human can never replace the company of others of its kind.

THE HATCHLINGS DEVELOP

In the wild, cockatiels can choose their life's companion from among many birds in a flock.

the egg right away—she'll simply lay another. Let her sit on the eggs for a while. This conserves her energy, because she will not produce more. If you have a pair of birds and prefer not to breed them, don't make a nest box available. If eggs appear anyway, prick them with a needle at both ends so the embryo will not develop, or replace the eggs with artificial ones.

The Hatchlings Develop

Newly hatched cockatiels have pink skin and yellow downy feathers. They cannot sit up, and their eyes are closed. They weigh about .2 oz (5 g). The parents feed their youngsters regurgitated food that is in a liquid form.

The chick's lower beak is wide, to catch the liquid. The upper beak still bears the egg tooth, which the

2 PROPER CARE AND FEEDING

chick used to break out of the shell.

After four or five days, the eyes begin to open and you can clearly hear the chicks cheeping for food. By now they weigh about .5 oz (15 g).

After ten days, the eyes are wide open. The first new tiny down feathers appear. The chick can raise its head and will hiss when disturbed. Now the parents begin to gradually replace the liquid regurgitated with a predigested seed regurgitant. The hungry youngsters bob eagerly as they beg for food. Each chick has grown to weigh about 1.25 oz (35 g).

After about fifteen days, the egg tooth drops off and the chicks can recognize their parents. They turn in the nest box to face the entry hole. The beak has hardened, and the chick weighs about 1.5–1.75 oz (40–50 g). The first quills emerge, showing the bird's coloring.

At eighteen days, the cheek patch appears. When a chick feels threatened, it will raise its crest, hiss, and spread its wings as a defensive measure.

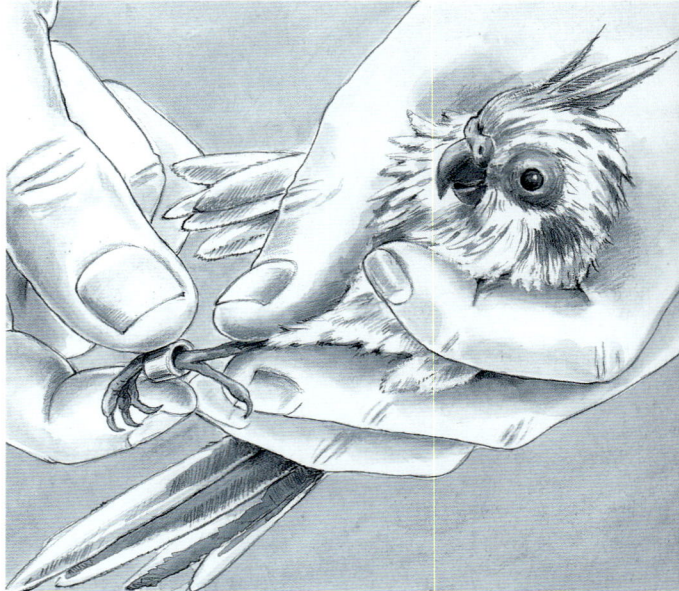

After 20 days or more, the yellow down feathers are replaced by gray. The chicks no longer look so bristly. They now weigh about 2.1 oz (60 g).

After 28 to 35 days, the plumage is complete, though the colors are more muted than in adults. Now the fledglings leave the nest.

They can fly right away, though they look wobbly and awkward.

Because they haven't mastered the skill of landing, they might fly straight

How to apply a closed leg band. Band your chicks when they are about seven days old.

86

HAND REARING

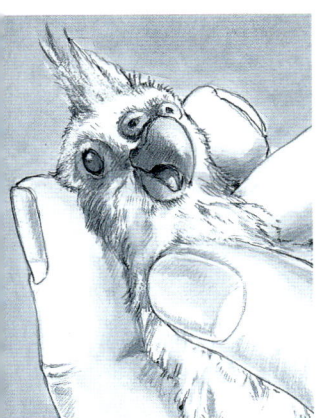

Feel the crop to determine whether the chick is getting enough to eat. In a healthy chick, the crop should be totally empty in the morning before the first feed of the day.

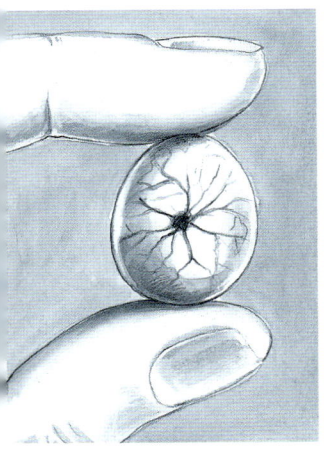

A fertilized egg, held against a flashlight.

into a wall and injure themselves.

At *about 35 to 40 days of age*, the youngsters begin to feed themselves, taking less and less food from their parents as they increasingly find it on their own.

Independence and Youth

Cockatiels tolerate the presence of their independent young. If the parents start a new brood, however, it's a good idea to move the juveniles to a separate aviary. To help them adjust, keep feeding them as you did in the breeding aviary. Don't forget vitamins, minerals, and trace elements (see page 65).

At *about six months of age*, the juveniles molt for the first time, acquiring their adult plumage. Now the sexes can be clearly distinguished.

At *nine months of age*, cockatiels are sexually mature, but you should wait a while before allowing them to breed.

Banding

When your chicks are about seven days old, you should band them. It takes practice to master the art of banding birds. Ask an experienced cockatiel breeder to show you how. Take the bird in one hand and hold one foot out gently. Carefully slide the band over the three longest toes, holding the fourth toe to the rear. Then push the ring up until it also slips over the fourth toe.

It is best to "close" band your birds. These bands are sturdier and a more permanent form of identification.

Hand Rearing

Rearing nestlings by hand is a challenge to be undertaken only in case of necessity, for example if both the parent birds should die.

Hand-reared cockatiels almost always "imprint" on the human who raises them, which typically makes them better pet birds. Although some feel that hand-reared birds may exhibit feather picking (see page 117), this is usually not the case. If possible, you can try placing the orphaned nestlings with suitable foster parents, but it is not necessary, as you can hand-feed them with some quick and easy training.

87

Observing and Understanding Cockatiels

If you take the time to observe your cockatiels and learn to interpret their behavior, you'll open the way to years of enjoyment.

3 OBSERVING AND UNDERSTANDING COCKATIELS

What Cockatiels Can Do

In order to see the range of cockatiel behavior in all its variety, you must keep at least two of the birds. If you make an effort to learn what their behavior means, keeping cockatiels can be a fascinating lesson in the ways of nature.

Behaviors You Should Recognize

Stretching the legs: The bird stretches one leg and the same wing as far behind it as it can, then pulls them back in, curling the toes at the same time. This motion is comparable to a person taking a stretch. It simply relaxes muscles that are fatigued.

Tucking the beak into the feathers on its back: This is the typical sleeping posture of many birds; the entire beak disappears into the fluffed-up feathers on the bird's back. It's amazing to see a cockatiel turn its head through 180 degrees. This also allows it to preen its back feathers easily.

Resting on one leg: This position takes the weight off the other leg. Birds also perch on one leg as they sleep. In the wild, this allows them to tuck one leg at a time up into the feathers for warmth in cold weather. For this reason, a bird that has lost a leg to injury or accident should not be kept in an outdoor aviary during the winter.

It's comical to watch a cockatiel stretch a leg way back, then bring it forward with a flourish before tucking it up out of sight again.

Lifting both wings: Likewise to relax the muscles, and also for exercise, a bird will lift and spread both wings. Cockatiels do this in very hot weather as well, to let cooler air waft against the body and allow body heat to escape. Finally, spreading the wings during a shower bath increases the amount of water that reaches the body surface.

Flapping its wings: If a bird holds tight to its perch and flaps both wings with vigor, it may be exercising its flight muscles or simply releasing excess energy.

Spreading both wings wide: This posture is part of the cock's mating ritual. He spreads his wings to impress his intended mate and to intimidate rivals by his size.

A flock of cockatiels in the wilds of Australia. This photo vividly shows why a solitary cockatiel is not likely to thrive in captivity.

BODY LANGUAGE

At the same time, the cock lowers his head and holds his tail high.

Grooming: By far the most common activity you'll observe is the cockatiels grooming and preening their feathers.

This behavior has already been described in detail elsewhere (see page 66).

Scratching: This is a normal everyday activity for

3 OBSERVING AND UNDERSTANDING COCKATIELS

Rose hips and leaves are high in vitamin A—and they also taste mighty good.

birds, serving to remove dirt from the feathers as well as to relieve any itching. A cockatiel can scratch its own head by bringing its foot up past its wings.

Note: A bird that scratches itself continually in the same spot should be taken to the veterinarian, as it may be infested with parasites (see page 74), or have a local bacterial infection in the skin.

Shaking out the feathers: Several times a day, especially in the morning, you will see your cockatiels shake out all their feathers. They do this with a vibrating motion all over the body. Shaking out the feathers like this gets rid of dust and puts the feathers in order.

This behavior can also be a sign of agitation. If danger threatens, each

BODY LANGUAGE

Why Do They Rub Their Beaks?

If you watch your cockatiel carefully, you will notice that it rubs its beak against a branch or a cuttlebone several times a day. One reason it does this is to remove food remnants such as bits of fruit or concentrated food from its beak. Another reason is to rub down any rough spots and keep its beak smooth. However, whetting its beak can also be a form of greeting. Answer your bird by scratching his perch with your fingernail. He will think you are a friend responding to him. And finally, it seems that a cockatiel may sometimes rub its beak because it finds itself in an awkward situation and doesn't know what else to do.

feather must be in its proper place so that the bird can take flight in time to escape.

Ruffling up the head feathers: The feathers on a cock's head, especially the yellow ones, are called its mask. The birds are able to ruffle up just these mask feathers so that each one stands up. You'll see this often in juveniles, who look even cuter with their feathers ruffled. In general, however, the mask feathers are ruffled when the bird is dozing or just before it falls asleep.

Fluffing up all the feathers: A bird can fluff up all its feathers so that each one stands erect. This traps an insulating layer of air between the skin and feathers all over the body. Cockatiels do this when they feel chilly, sometimes even in their sleep. If you see a bird with its feathers fluffed up all day long, you should be concerned; it might be sick (see page 73).

Yawning: All psittacine birds yawn from time to time. As in people, this is usually a sign that the bird needs to take a deep breath, is mildly oxygen depleted, and therefore feels tired.

Sneezing: A cockatiel's sneeze sounds remarkably like a human's. Usually, however, sneezing doesn't mean that the bird has a cold, for then it would also have a runny nose. A cockatiel's normal sneeze is just a way of clearing out its nostrils, as we do by sniffing.

3 OBSERVING AND UNDERSTANDING COCKATIELS

Speech Sounds

The sounds cockatiels use to communicate with each other are relatively quiet. There are sounds for anxiety, for courtship, for begging food from the parents, for staying in contact during flight—and, of course, there are the random shrieks. Although the individual chirps and coos are soft, a monotonous repetition or constant calls from birds left on their own can be quite a nuisance. It's important to determine the reason for this behavior and try to remedy the situation.

What the Crest Indicates

Relaxation: In all normal, calm, and relaxed situations, the cockatiel's crest lies almost horizontal to the head. The tips of the crest point up, and the feathers are completely smooth (see top illustration on this page).

Interest: When the bird engages in activities that require its attention, responds alertly to something that attracts its interest, or curiously examines something new, the crest stands erect (see bottom illustration on this page).

Tension: If the crest is extremely erect, almost pointing forward, this is a sign of great agitation and tension as well as extreme concentration (see bottom illustration, facing page).

Anxiety: When anxious, uncertain, or fearful, the cockatiel lays its crest back and hisses. It also juts its head forward (see top illustration, facing page).

Cockatiels Are Clever

Because cockatiels, like budgerigars and zebra finches, have been kept by humans as pets for a long time, they are considered to be domesticated. However, they have retained some of their wild ways, including traits that make them good indoor birds.

There is almost no creature with as much curiosity as a pet cockatiel. Any novelty is examined thoroughly. In the wild, this serves to help the bird notice and adapt to new factors and changing conditions in its environment.

In captivity, however, this curiosity can lead to

Top: The crest lies flat, a sign that the bird is calm and relaxed.

Bottom: If something arouses the cockatiel's interest, the crest stands erect.

COCKATIELS ARE CLEVER

Top: With beak opened wide, the bird hisses a threat.

Bottom: The stiff, erect crest indicates extreme agitation.

Right: Sleeping, the cockatiel tucks its head into the feathers on its back.

3 OBSERVING AND UNDERSTANDING COCKATIELS

comical or even dangerous situations.

For example, if your cockatiel is nearby when you flush the toilet, it will look with interest to see where the water is coming from. If it perches on the toilet and leans too far over, it might fall in and could even drown.

Any new object will first get a thorough visual inspection, and then be explored with beak or tongue. This means that the head and beak are especially vulnerable to injury (from burning candles, electric irons, and so forth).

If certain activities are repeated with regularity, the bird soon learns to take advantage.

For example, it won't be long before a cockatiel knows where the cage door is. If the door is latched, it will thoroughly investigate the latch and possibly even open it with its beak.

A pair of cockatiels will call without interruption to maintain voice contact when they are apart. In the wild, this helps them to find each other again. You can take advantage of this behavior if one bird escapes. Set the other in its cage by an open window; the fugitive will often return to its mate.

The Senses

Smell: It's likely that birds

Lifting the wings is a sign that the bird is trying to cool down, or perhaps just to relax its muscles.

THE SENSES

TIP

It's easy to determine that a cockatiel can taste a salty flavor. These birds eagerly go after foods containing salt. A bit of salty pretzel may add a little variety to the bird's diet. But be very careful; too much is dangerous and will cause salt toxicity, which could result in death. In the wild, birds get salt by eating dirt that contains minerals.

A cockatiel stands at rest on the ground.

can detect various odors. We do know that birds perceive odors and can use this sense to locate food and to navigate.

Taste: Birds do have taste buds, although they are lower in number than those found in mammals. In the wild, parents teach their young which foods are easily digestible, and birds also learn by experience. Probing first with the tongue, the cockatiel will reject a substance that is inedible. As pets, on the other hand, a bird is offered a wide range of foods and may develop preferences for one or another, depending on its taste.

Hearing: Cockatiels have a well-developed sense of hearing. Good hearing is important in the wild, where the birds must communicate over long distances. For example, a bird can warn the flock from far away when a predator threatens.

Sight: Sight is the most highly developed of most birds' senses, and it far surpasses that of mammals. Because the eyes are positioned at the sides of the head, cockatiels can see almost all around them. On the other hand, the region visible to both eyes at once is quite limited. However, birds can see five times as many images in one second as humans. This is very important, above all, during swift flight. In the wild, the creature that identifies an enemy sooner has a longer life.

The ability to see colors is strong in birds. This is essential, especially in foraging for food and in identifying enemies (recognizing the warning markings of many species of snakes and insects, for example).

OBSERVING AND UNDERSTANDING COCKATIELS

Building Trust, Step by Step

If you and your new cockatiels are to live in harmony, it's important that they learn to trust you. For this reason, take great care as you introduce them to their new home. Spend a lot of time preparing their cage, so that their first hours in their new home will be minimally stressful. Making them feel welcome and safe encourages them to be tame and friendly rather than timid and wary.

The Trip Home
When you pick up your cockatiels from the breeder or pet store, they will probably be placed in a small wooden or cardboard box. This ensures that they are safe from drafts.

BUILDING TRUST

Tempted by a tasty snack, the cockatiel overcomes its natural wariness of your hand.

The smooth walls inside the box protect them from injury, and the darkness and quiet help to keep them calm.

Bring your cockatiels home by the fastest route. If the weather is very hot or very cold, take additional precautions to keep the birds comfortable.

When you arrive at home, you'll want to put the birds in their new cage right away. It's essential to have everything ready ahead of time.

Building Trust

Leaving the birds in the travel box, open its door next to the opened door of the cage, making sure that the only way out of the box leads into the cage. Wait until the birds emerge on their own; this might take several minutes.

Don't rush the birds by rapping on the box or reaching inside. They are already unsettled by their journey, and they will associate you with their negative experience. Also, a cockatiel's bite can be fierce.

Once the birds have entered their cage, close its door and then keep your distance. On their first day in their new home, the cockatiels should be left in peace to take in their new surroundings. A pair of birds will adjust somewhat more readily than a solitary bird.

The first few days are the hardest, both for you and for the birds. If you need to approach the cage, for example to fill the feed

A tame cockatiel delights in having its head scratched.

99

3 OBSERVING AND UNDERSTANDING COCKATIELS

What Pleases or Distresses Cockatiels

What Pleases a Cockatiel

- Lots of attention from its owner or another cockatiel.
- A tasty morsel now and then as a reward.
- Branches and twigs to gnaw on (see page 44).
- Plenty of exercise and opportunity for free flight.
- Voice contact with its keeper, in a low conversational tone.
- Affectionate scratching by its mate or a favorite person.
- Familiar arrangement of cage equipment.
- Familiar surroundings in its flying territory.
- Familiar appearance of its keeper (clothing, hairstyle, and so on).
- High vantage points during free flight; cage elevated for a sense of security.
- Continual entertainment and activity to prevent boredom.

What Distresses a Cockatiel

- Prolonged periods of solitude.
- Sudden appearance of a person who has approached the cage without speaking.
- Anything new in its environment (introduce changes gradually).
- New toys and cage furnishings. Let the bird get used to these from a distance first.
- Loud, unfamiliar noises.
- Constant vibrations and shaking. For example, don't set the cage on top of the refrigerator.
- Being grabbed and held.
- Being chased, whether by its keeper, by other household pets, or by children.
- Drafts or prolonged cold temperatures.
- Lack of routine in its daily schedule.
- A dry environment without any way to bathe or shower.

cups, move slowly and calmly. If possible, follow the same routine each time.

New events, sudden movements, and noise will alarm your birds.

If the cockatiels are very timid, sit down far enough away from the cage that they aren't agitated. Then talk quietly to them. The words don't matter—what's important is the tone of your voice.

As you speak, call your cockatiels by the names you have chosen for them. They will soon learn to

BUILDING TRUST

connect these names with themselves.

Slowly, the cockatiels will learn to trust you. Then it's safe to move closer to the cage.

Taming Cockatiels

Over the next several days, gradually spend more time near the cage, talking calmly to the cockatiels. Finally, you will be able to stand right beside the cage without alarming the birds. Now you can begin—slowly and carefully—to tame the cockatiels to your touch.

First, rest your hand gently on the cage itself; a little later, extend your hand through the open door and into the cage. Once the birds have learned that your hand is not a threat to them, you can take the next steps towards building trust. Hold your hand close to a bird, touch it lightly, then gently stroke its belly feathers. You might want to place a bit of millet spray or other delicacy on your outstretched hand. Move your hand slowly under the cockatiel's belly and say the words "step up." Usually this is enough to encourage it to step onto your finger. Soothing words and treats in moderation help to overcome any wariness on the bird's part. To put the bird down, move your finger towards the place you want the bird to

When your cockatiel is so tame that it will step onto your outstretched finger of its own accord, it's very easy to return the bird to its cage after free flight.

OBSERVING AND UNDERSTANDING COCKATIELS

step down to and say "step down."

Repeat this process inside the cage until you are sure that each bird will willingly climb onto your hand whenever you like.

Now you can let your cockatiels out for their first free flight.

If a bird is still timid, getting it back into the cage will call for patience on your part. Don't try to chase it down and capture it; this would only destroy whatever trust it has already learned. As always, avoid any rapid movements in the bird's presence. In some cases, darkening the room a bit will help encourage a bird to step onto your waiting hand for its return to the cage.

Nighttime Rest

Cockatiels usually divide their days into periods of activity and rest on their own, although they also will adjust to the daily rhythm of the household.

At night, the birds definitely need their rest. Once your cockatiels have settled onto their accustomed sleeping perches, you should not disturb them. It's a good idea to leave a dim nightlight burning, so the birds can orient themselves should they be alarmed by something and wake up in the dark of night. It's not necessary to cover the cage with a cloth.

First Free Flight

Once the cockatiels have shown that they are not afraid to come to your hand, it's time for their first free flight.

Precautions to take:
■ Be absolutely sure that all doors and windows are closed and any potential hazards are eliminated (see page 54).
■ Close the curtains at the windows and glass doors. Cockatiels are swift fliers and do not understand glass. If a cockatiel collides with a windowpane, it may break its neck and die. Over time, you can gradually pull the curtains back or raise the blinds, increasing the exposed glass surface little by little.

Now it's time: Open the cage door and let the birds decide for themselves when to venture forth. Under no

TIP
▼

Never place your hand on the roof of the cage while the cockatiels are inside, and try never to grasp a bird from above in your hand. The cockatiel will react with instinctive alarm, for in the wild its greatest natural enemies are birds of prey that strike from above. Any beginnings of trust your cockatiels have developed towards you will be lost in an instant.

These two have become great friends. The cockatiel nuzzles the boy's cheek, trying to get as close to him as possible.

FIRST FREE FLIGHT

circumstances should you try to chase an unwilling cockatiel out of its safe haven in the cage.

Likewise, you should allow the birds to return to their cage on their own. The decision is an easy one if a bird is hungry.

At the beginning, many birds have difficulty in landing. Belly flops and crash landings can be very dangerous, and can cause the bird to fracture its distal vertebrae or pygostyle. Birds with such a fracture cannot raise their tails and posture to defecate. This leads to a pasted or solid vent area. Birds with this problem need veterinary attention immediately. Over time, the birds will come to prefer certain perches about the room. If you spread newspapers under these perches, it will be easier to clean up the inevitable droppings.

3 OBSERVING AND UNDERSTANDING COCKATIELS

Fun and Games with Cockatiels

The mental skills of a cockatiel might not compete with the intelligence of a parrot, but they easily match those of other domesticated birds. To keep these skills sharp, it's a very good idea to have at least two cockatiels living together and to give them ample space to develop their personalities. For a singly kept bird, the human owner becomes an essential substitute companion. This means that you must devote a considerable amount of time and attention to the cockatiel in your care.

Companionship Is Key

Because cockatiels are quite clever and extremely convivial birds, the worst thing you can do is to leave them alone for long periods without entertainment or mental stimulation.

When you are at home, you should share your daily routine with the birds as a matter of course. Companionship is the essential element in the life of cockatiels. Pay attention to what they like and dislike (see table, page 100). This will help you to understand the personality and behavior of your little charges.

For example, if a bird is afraid of the vacuum cleaner, you can talk soothingly to it and place it in its cage, where it feels safe. The cockatiel will soon learn that it is not in danger, and it will often retreat to the cage on its own when the vacuum cleaner appears on the scene.

Daily household chores can be an endless source of entertainment and activity. Time to set the table? Many cockatiels love to push the knives and forks onto the floor. If you're not worried about the silverware, it can be fun to watch the little imps at their tricks. On the other hand, if a bird does something it

Even a large leaf of lettuce can entertain a cockatiel for a while.

FUN AND GAMES WITH COCKATIELS

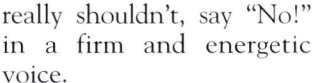

Playing with jewelry, however, can be dangerous to a cockatiel.

really shouldn't, say "No!" in a firm and energetic voice.

More often than not, the cockatiel will stop its mischief at your command.

A very tame cockatiel loves to ride about on "its" person's shoulder. This puts it right in the middle of the action.

Many birds will let you carry them to the faucet at the sink, where they will enjoy a little shower in the running water.

Another favorite activity for cockatiels is to play with several large marbles on a tabletop, pushing them so they roll and bump each other. Both noise and motion seem to be extremely entertaining for these birds.

■ Make a tassel out of hemp to amuse your pet. Cut about 20 strips of natural-colored hemp, each 6 in (15 cm) long. Tie the strips together at the center, then bend them in

105

3 OBSERVING AND UNDERSTANDING COCKATIELS

half. Knot another strip of hemp tightly around the bundle, about 0.8 in (2 cm) down from the center point.

Hang the resulting tassel with a loop of hemp in the cage or on the climbing tree. Your cockatiels will have fun tugging the strips from the bundle one by one.

■ Play "catch" with your cockatiel, using a small ball with openings for gripping. Place the ball on the table; the bird will soon discover how to take the ball in its beak and throw it. Your part in this little game is to retrieve the ball and roll it back to the bird for another toss.

■ Although bells are often sold in pet shops as play toys for birds, they are metal and could contain lead and zinc, especially in the clapper. Zinc and lead can kill your bird, so any toys made of metal should be stainless steel only.

■ Send your cockatiel on a food hunt. For example, crumple a piece of ink-free paper around a piece of millet spray to form a ball. As the bird plays with the ball, the paper will open to surprise the cockatiel with a yummy treat. Or hide the sprig of millet in a small cardboard box. Cut some small slits in the box to give the bird a starting point. The cockatiel will eagerly work away with its beak until it can get at the tasty morsel inside.

■ Tame cockatiels like to play the ladder game. As the bird perches on your forefinger, hold your other hand in front of it, with that forefinger slightly higher. Your cockatiel will keep hopping briskly from one finger to the next as you alternate hands.

Guinea pigs and cockatiels usually get along just fine.

FUN AND GAMES WITH COCKATIELS

This inviting perch also serves as a climbing ladder or a swing.

This amusing game also provides good exercise.

■ Read the newspaper with your cockatiel. Rustle the pages to attract its interest. If you tear one page halfway down, your birds will enjoy ripping it the rest of the way and then shredding the paper to bits.

■ Float a few grapes in a shallow bowl of water. Place the cockatiel on the edge of the bowl and watch it go to work to capture the bobbing fruit with its beak.

■ Many cockatiels enjoy classical music or other tunes. Observe how your birds react to music. They may even learn to imitate the melody (see page 110).

■ Test your cockatiel's intelligence. For example, take two small dishes that look different. Put water in one dish and a treat such as millet in the other. Cover each dish with a coaster or a piece of cardboard. You'll be amazed at how quickly your birds will learn to identify the dish that holds the delicious reward.

Scientists have developed a way to test the intelligence of parrots that you can easily carry out with your own cockatiels at home.

Cockatiels can distinguish colors (see page 97). Place birdseed in one of two identical dishes and cover it with a piece of green cardboard. Cover the other dish with red cardboard. Let the bird watch as you cover the two dishes.

Now show the cockatiel another piece of the same green cardboard that covers the dish containing food.

The bird will soon learn what it must do. It will hop over to the dish covered with green cardboard, tug with its beak to remove the lid, and help itself to a well-earned and very tasty snack.

3 OBSERVING AND UNDERSTANDING COCKATIELS

The Right Toys

You will not always have time to play with your cockatiels. If you give them appropriate toys, however, they can entertain themselves quite nicely.

The climbing tree is often a favorite playground, especially if it is hung with toys as well (see page 56).

Of course, the birds should have access to the climbing tree only when you are at home to supervise.

If they are left out on their own, unexpected accidents may lead to injury. Never leave a bird alone and out of its cage.

Suitable toys for cockatiels are sold in pet stores, but you can also make them yourself. Popular items include wooden rings and ladders, as well as beads or empty spools strung together on a cord.

Even something as simple as a natural branch to gnaw on can entertain cockatiels for hours.

Other inexpensive sources of entertainment are cardboard boxes, empty toilet paper rolls, and scraps of paper, which cockatiels will spend hours reducing to confetti. Be careful about printed paper, however, as the ink may be toxic.

A thicker cord or rope, knotted and suspended in the cage, invites gymnastics. It's important to be watchful that the birds don't unravel it, pulling out fibers that they might swallow. This could cause problems in the crop or the rest of the digestive system.

Cockatiels love anything that glitters. This

Working for an edible reward provides fun and exercise.

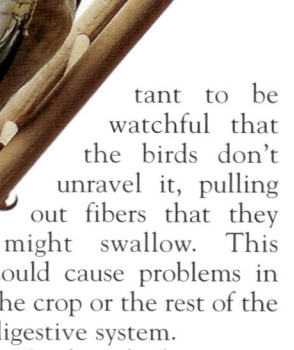

SPEECH LESSONS

Cockatiel Tricks

Cockatiels are clever creatures. Susan has observed this with her two birds, Mini and Maxi. She lets her birds fly about the room every day. Before long, Mini and Maxi discovered a wall lamp with a small cord hanging from it. The cockatiels soon learned how to tug the cord with their beaks to turn on the light. Of course, the two birds also answer to their own names. When Susan calls them, they land on her shoulder and let her carry them around the house. In the kitchen, they fly straight to the sink. Cocking their little heads, they look encouragingly at Susan. Obediently, she turns the water on so they can have a shower. They take turns spreading their wings and splashing under the gentle stream. But Mini and Maxi have also learned that some activities are forbidden. For example, if Susan catches them nibbling on the curtains, she says "Stop that!" in a loud, firm voice. Immediately, the two rascals take to their wings. What's more, Susan's cockatiels are resourceful—they quickly learned how to open their cage door and let themselves out for a bit of fun. Now the door has a safety latch.

includes a ballpoint pen or your jewelry (see photo, page 105). They will also gnaw on pencils, but be careful—ink cartridges and lead pencils are toxic to birds. Absolutely no type of pencil is safe for a cockatiel to chew.

Note: If your cockatiels lose interest in a particular plaything, remove it from the cage for several days. When you put it back, it will be like a new toy.

Speech Lessons

If your heart is set on owning a bird that's a talented conversationalist, repeating everything it hears, then a cockatiel is not necessarily the best choice.

Many other species of birds, including gray parrots and mynah birds, are much better at such mimicry. However, even cockatiels can learn to imitate certain sounds.

Mimicking musical notes or even entire melodies comes easily to many cockatiels. To help them master this skill, play or whistle the same tune over and over again for your birds. Continue the repetition

3 OBSERVING AND UNDERSTANDING COCKATIELS

until the birds can reproduce the melody perfectly. Because warbling is part of the cock's courtship behavior as he tries to impress the hen, males are often better than females at repeating a given melody.

Imitating speech is less common in a cockatiel's repertoire of tricks. However, you might try to discover and promote a hidden talent among your birds.

Here too, the key is regular repetition of the words you want the bird to learn. Practice with your cockatiel as often as you can. It's important to use the same tone of voice and to recite exactly the same words in the same situations. Your bird will learn best if you proceed gradually. Once it has mastered a certain word or phrase—such as "good morning!"—you can repeat that one less often and begin teaching a new word.

Always be sure the cockatiel isn't distracted by other noises or activities during its lesson.

It's a good idea to practice with the bird perched on your hand in a slightly darkened room. This helps the cockatiel to concentrate. Don't demand too much, however.

If a lesson isn't going very well, don't lose patience and give up. Do something else for a while, then make a fresh start at another time.

Note: If it turns out that your cockatiels aren't gifted at talking, or even at imitating melodies, don't hold this against them. Instead, take delight in their other endearing tricks.

Observing Your Feathered Friends

Try these suggestions for an interesting view of the var-

A swing from the pet store adds variety to the cage or climbing tree.

OBSERVING YOUR FEATHERED FRIENDS

ious expressive positions of a cockatiel's crest (see page 94).

Hang a new plaything in your cockatiels' cage. For best results, choose a toy with especially gaudy colors.

At first, the bird will view the new object with suspicion, often even hissing at it. When it's clear that no danger exists, the cockatiel will investigate the new object with its beak and tongue, chirping softly all the while.

Similar behavior is evident when the birds are enjoying free flight and notice something different in their surroundings. Such changes bring variety to the birds' daily lives and can be entertaining for you as well. Too many changes from day to day can be stressful, however, because the birds don't have a chance to become accustomed to the new situation.

It is important to keep the level of change to a minimum with any pet bird, and especially with curious, active, and playful cockatiels. Changes in the bird's environment can elicit stress. Stressed birds may become ill, begin feather picking, or even die. Birds are very susceptible to stress and they need to know that their cage, their haven, is a safe, familiar place.

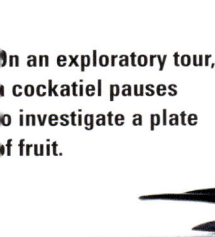

On an exploratory tour, a cockatiel pauses to investigate a plate of fruit.

Problems and How to Solve Them

A cockatiel keeper should be aware of problems that may arise. Most problems are caused by improper care or a lack of information about what the cockatiels need.

Fear of Touch

Situation: A newly acquired cockatiel won't become hand-tame, even though the owner devotes considerable time and attention to the bird.

Possible causes: A young cockatiel may have had very bad experiences with humans, or the new pet may not be a young bird at all, but an older cockatiel that has been separated from its mate.

Remedy: You might try using very gentle force to teach the bird not to be afraid of human touch. Place a favorite food on your open hand, then set the bird on your hand as well, holding it loosely with your other hand. You should not wear gloves, because that would make the bird even more fearful. This method is advisable only for the brave and hardy few, because a cockatiel's bite can be fierce. If you manage to repeat this process over several days, most timid cockatiels will learn that they have nothing to fear from your touch.

Introducing a New Cockatiel

Situation: A bird that has been kept alone is placed in a cage with another cockatiel, but the two birds evidently don't get along.

Possible causes: One of the birds had a longtime partner and doesn't want a new mate. It's also possible that a bird learned to view a human as its partner. In that case, it won't accept another cockatiel as a suitable companion.

Remedy: As natural flock-dwellers, cockatiels are usually quite tolerant. If you want to place a single cockatiel with another of its kind, you should start the birds in two cages side by side, then later place the birds together in a spacious cages and observe their behavior very closely. If there is no strife in the first few hours, they will probably continue to get along.

If they object to each other at the start, put them in two adjacent cages again. Give them their first free flight together in neutral territory—a room that is unfamiliar to both of them. If they tolerate each other reasonably well, place them in a roomy cage again, if possible an unfamiliar one, also in a room that is new to both birds. Give them food only in this common cage. This method of getting them used to each other usually works quite well. In this situation, the sex of the two birds is usually not a factor; even birds of the same sex will get along fine.

Dull, Listless Bird

Situation: The cockatiel doesn't move about much, has little appetite, and is quiet.

Possible causes: Your first thought should be that the cockatiel may be sick, or possibly nesting, or possibly lonely.

PROBLEMS AND HOW TO SOLVE THEM

Remedy: First try to determine why the bird's behavior has changed, taking corrective measures as needed. Also check to see that there's nothing wrong with its food. Watch the cockatiel closely for no more than an hour, looking for any signs of illness (see page 73). If the bird gets weaker, seems sleepy, and stops eating altogether, take it to the veterinarian at once.

Changes in the Feces

Situation: The droppings lose their slightly solid consistency and become runny or even liquid. The clear, white, and green portions of the excrement are no longer distinct.

Possible causes: It may be that the cockatiel ate a lot of fruit, drank too much water, or that the bird was extremely agitated. In all these cases, changes in the feces are not uncommon, though only one or two sets of droppings should be affected before they return to normal.

Remedy: Provide fresh food and water. If the excrement has not returned to its normal consistency within a short time, take the bird to the veterinarian right away (see page 76).

Blood on the Vent

Situation: The bird strains to void droppings, but without success. In many cases, the feathers around the cloacal vent are bloody and the underbelly appears swollen.

Possible causes: Sometimes a bird that eats paper will become constipated. Other possibilities include egg binding in females, a benign fatty tumor, or a malignant growth.

Remedy: Consult a veterinarian immediately.

Skin Changes and Injuries

Situation: You notice a little bleeding or a change in the cockatiel's skin.

Possible causes: The bird may have cut or bruised itself by colliding with something during free flight or while cavorting about its cage or the climbing tree.

Remedy: Dab small wounds with a gauze to stop

You and your cockatiel may be the best of friends, but you should not share a drinking glass.

OBSERVING AND UNDERSTANDING COCKATIELS

the bleeding. Then disinfect with betadine. Deep wounds must be treated by the veterinarian (see page 73).

Frequent Yawning or Sneezing

Situation: A bird whose behavior is otherwise normal seems to yawn quite often, or sneezes without any nasal discharge.

Possible causes: In general, yawning indicates either fatigue or a lack of sufficient oxygen. Sneezing, if the bird is healthy, is often a sign of dry, dusty air or of nasal congestion. However, yawning and/or sneezing could be signs of disease and an avian veterinarian should be consulted.

Remedy: Provide fresh, clean air. Ventilate the bird's room often, but avoid causing drafts. If the bird has had lots of exercise, a little snooze will do it good. Humidifiers or indoor fountains provide moisture and help prevent nasal congestion. If the bird's nostrils are clogged, take it to the veterinarian to have them cleaned out.

What if a Bird Loses Its Mate?

When a cockatiel chooses a mate, it has found a lifelong companion. Benjamin had a pair of cockatiels for several years, and then the female died. Benjamin could tell that the male missed his partner very much. The little cock stopped chirping as it had in the past, and it did not want to leave its cage. To console his pet, Benjamin spent extra time talking to it, stroking and scratching it, and offering it toys and treats. After a while, the cockatiel gradually became more lively and cheerful again. If a young bird loses its mate, there is a chance that it will become attached to a new companion (see page 112).

Excess Dropping of Feathers

Situation: Many loose feathers lie about the cage.

Possible causes: The possible causes are many and varied. In the so-called shock molt, a bird drops many feathers all at once out of fear or to escape a predator. If the feathers fall out over several days, the bird may have a metabolic disorder, a hormone problem, or a nutritional deficiency.

Remedy: It is necessary to consult a veterinarian for diagnosis. Close examination of dropped feathers may help determine why they fell out.

A variety of healthy foods, such as a commercial pelleted diet and fresh fruits and vegetables, as well as adequate natural or artificial sunlight, support good feather growth.

PROBLEMS AND HOW TO SOLVE THEM

Guarding One Leg or Wing

Situation: The cockatiel uses only one leg when perching, or is unable to fly because it cannot move one wing properly or at all.

Possible causes: The problem could be anything from a bruise to a broken bone.

Remedy: If the bird can move and use the limb, it is probably not broken, but merely bruised. You should take the bird to the veterinarian regardless.

If the limb hangs limply or the bird can't move it, you must take the cockatiel to the veterinarian immediately, as the limb is probably broken and will need to be radiographed.

Quarrels in the Aviary

Situation: Cockatiels are introduced to an aviary that is already occupied by a breeding pair. The pair responds aggressively to the newcomers.

Cause: The breeding pair is unable to establish its own small territory within the aviary.

Remedy: It's not a good idea to confront a breeding pair with newcomers of its species. The aggressive behavior of the soon-to-be-parent birds might jeopardize any chance of communal life among the flock. In any aviary, be sure that there is enough room for each breeding pair to have its own separate territory. Always be sure the flock contains an equal number of males and females. If you keep more than one pair of birds, have enough nest boxes to give each pair a choice.

The Bird Is Too Fat

Situation: A cockatiel gradually gains so much weight that it can hardly fly.

Causes: Cockatiels will get fat especially when they are fed an improper diet, like a seed mix, eat too much of a single food, like sunflower seeds, or don't get enough exercise.

Many cockatiels develop a preference for sunflower seeds, which

Seizing the moment—the bread disappears while nobody's watching.

OBSERVING AND UNDERSTANDING COCKATIELS

are typically contained in ready-mixed bird feed. These seeds have a high fat content and tend to be addictive.

Remedy: Conversion to a pelleted commercial bird food with up to 15 percent fruits and vegetables is best, but this sort of diet must be introduced very slowly and gradually, or the cockatiel that was on a seed diet before might die. If the bird is addicted to sunflower seeds, remove them from the diet. Offer more fruits and vegetables. Offer smaller seeds, like millet, or canary grass seed, or safflower seeds.

Many birds have a tendency to eat only their favorite foods. If you, as their keeper, give in to their preferences and offer a cockatiel only the seeds that it particularly likes, the bird's diet is bound to be unbalanced. If the bird will not convert to a commercial pelleted diet, a safflower seed mix offered with fresh fruits and vegetables is the next best choice.

Because nuts of any kind are also very high in fat, the amount of nuts in your birds' diet should be kept to a minimum.

Note: It's rare to find overweight birds in an aviary or a large cage containing several birds. The birds stimulate each other to exercise more, and they will even scuffle over who will have the best place at the feeding dish. As a result, their bodies don't have the chance to store fat.

A better way to help a bird lose weight is to provide plenty of exercise along with a varied and balanced diet.

As a treat or a reward, a half or quarter of a nut serves the same purpose as a whole one.

Molting

Situation: The bird loses individual feathers all year long.

Cause: Molt is the term used to describe the regular change of a bird's plumage. It is not a disease condition, but a natural process. If a bird lost all its feathers at once, it would be unable to fly. In the wild, it would soon fall victim to preda-

Don't offer greens unless you're sure they have not been sprayed.

tors. Parrotlike birds such as cockatiels molt continuously almost all year long. Therefore, it's not unusual to see a few feathers here and there in the cage.

In shock molt, the bird actually sheds a number of feathers all at once as protection against an imminent attack.

Mild metabolic disorders, more often seen in older birds, may cause abnormal molting. If this happens, take the bird to a veterinarian.

Molting can stress a bird's body, because it takes energy to form new feathers. As a rule, however, rest and a balanced diet are all that a bird needs to molt without major problems. For older birds, an infrared lamp can be helpful (see page 73).

Feather Picking

Situation: The cockatiel has almost no feathers, except on its head region. The bird has plucked them all out.

Possible causes: This problem occurs mostly in large parrots, but cockatiels may also be affected. The causes are nutritional, infectious, metabolic, physical, or emotional. Emotional disturbances are most commonly involved, particularly in singly kept or very tame birds.

Remedy: Once a bird has started picking its feathers, it's very difficult to break the habit, even if the original cause, such as a skin disease, has long been remedied. First, consult an avian veterinarian to identify and eliminate any physical, metabolic, infectious, or nutritional causes.

Once your avian veterinarian has examined and tested your bird and determined that its problem is an emotional one, you must look for an emotional cause. What has changed?

Carefully examine the recent history of your household. Have there been any changes at all? Any change could be significant: a new pet, a new baby, a new significant other, new carpet, new wallpaper, etc. All of these things could upset your bird and cause it to feather pick.

Try to comfort your bird, spend more time with it,

PROBLEMS AND HOW TO SOLVE THEM

and be consistent. Greet your bird each time you come into your home and each morning when you wake up. Say good-bye to your bird each time you leave your home, and good night before you go to bed. Give your bird its meals and treats on schedule. Buy your bird new toys; and perhaps move its cage into a more active area of your home. Take your bird out of its cage more often and play with it.

If environmental changes do not work, then discuss the use of a collar to thwart your bird from feather picking. Also discuss mood altering drugs with your avian veterinarian. The drugs may give your bird the new outlook on life it needs.

Note: Deformed and discolored feathers may be diseased, or may have arisen from a problem for which there is no treatment. Defective feathers can be removed by an avian veterinarian, and evaluated histologically. Structural, infectious, and viral feather abnormalities can be determined by microscopic examination of the feather, its shaft, and its pulp.

117

OF GENERAL IMPORTANCE

My Cockatiels

Place a favorite photo here.

_____
Name

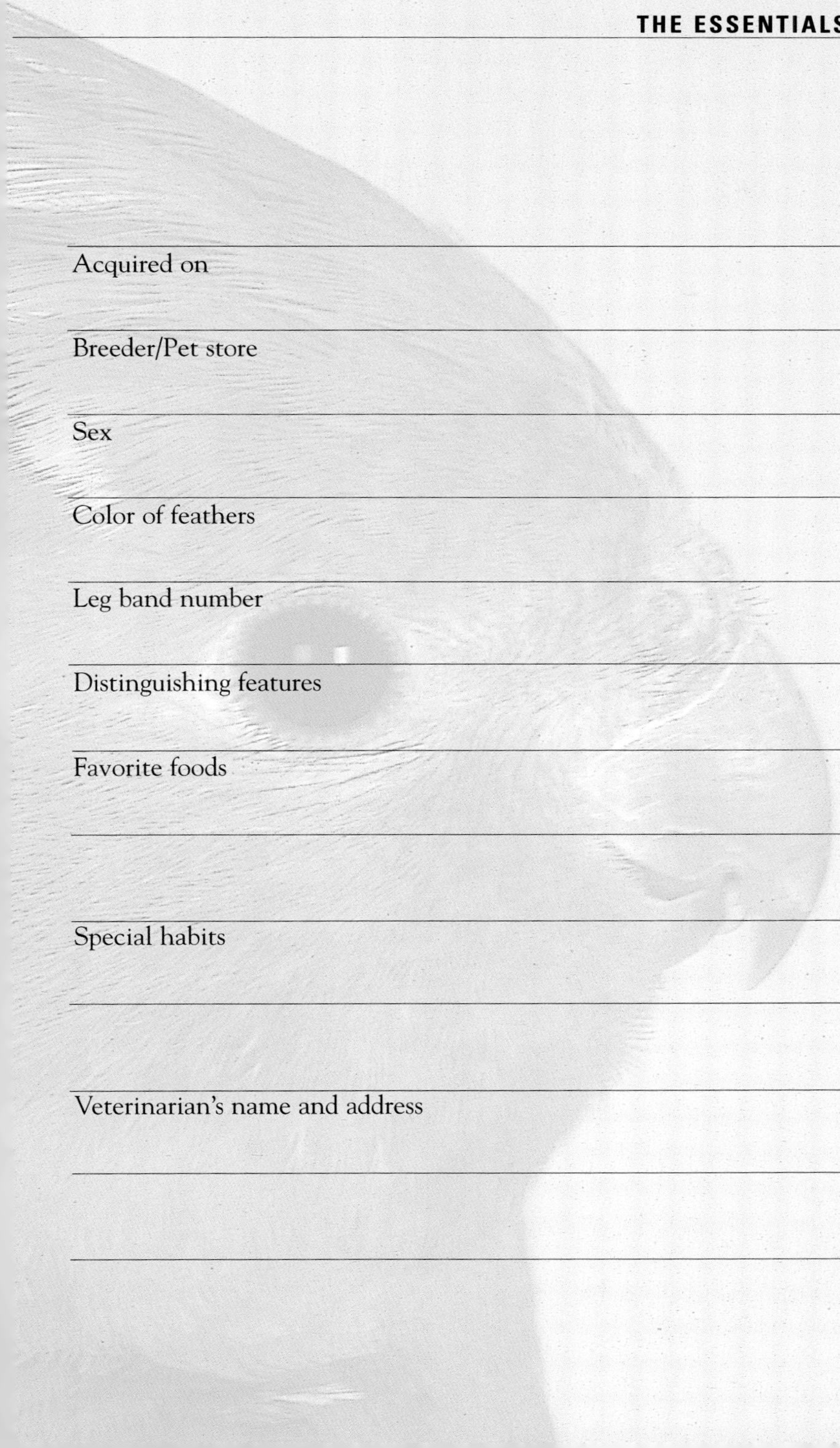

THE ESSENTIALS AT A GLANCE

Acquired on

Breeder/Pet store

Sex

Color of feathers

Leg band number

Distinguishing features

Favorite foods

Special habits

Veterinarian's name and address

OF GENERAL IMPORTANCE

Accessories, 48–49
Activities, 104–111
Albino Cockatiel, 34, **37**
Apartment living, 26–27
Appearance, 13–14
Appliances, 54
Australia, 8, 90
Automatic feed/water dispensers, 47
Aviaries, 43–44
  indoor, 43–44
  outdoor, 44
  quarrels in, 115

Banding, 27, **86**, 87
Bathing, 67–68
Beak, 14
  trimming, 75–76
Behaviors, 90–97
Bells, 106
Birdbath, 42–43
Bird-proofing a room, 51–52
Body, 13
Body temperature, 73
Breeders, 28
Breeding, 26–27
  for color, 15–16
  courtship, **80**, 81–82
  egg laying, 84–85
  essentials for, 80–81
  hatchlings, 85–87

pairing, 82–83
  time, 12
Brooding, 83
Burrowing mites, 74
Buying, tips for, 28–33
  a healthy cockatiel, 30–32
  making a choice, 28–29
  where to buy, 28
  why a young bird, 29–30

Cage, 42, **45**. *See also* Aviaries
  accessories for, 48–49
  cleaning, 70
  placement of, 50–51
Calcium, 47
Catch, playing, 106
Cats, 24
Children and cockatiels, 24–25
Chlamydia, 71
Chlamydiosis, 79
Cinnamon Cockatiel, 34, **36**
Claw trimming, 75–76
Climate, 8–9
Climbing tree, 56–57
  cleaning, 57
  how to build, 57
  materials for, 56–57
Cloaca, 76
Clothing, 54
Cock, 20

Cockatiels. *See also* Wild cockatiels
  activities for, 104–111
  behaviors of, 90–97
  breeding, 15–16, 80–87
  building trust, 99–101
  buying tips, 28–33
  considerations before purchase, 18, 20, 22–25
  domestication, 14
  housing and accessories, 43–49
  hygiene for, 66–71
  illnesses and preventive care, 72–79
  Latin name, 14–15
  pleasing vs. distressing things, 100
  problems and solutions, 112–117
  senses of, 96–97
  trip home, 98–99
Coloration, 15–16
  albino, 34
  cinnamon, 34
  lutino, 34
  pearled, 34
  pied, 34
  silver, 34
  white face, 34
Companionship, 104
Concussion, 78–79
Considerations before purchase, 18, 20, 22–25
Constipation, 76

120

INDEX

Containers, 54
Courting song, 82
Courtship, **80**, 81–82
Crest, **94**, 94
Crop stasis, 78
Curiosity, 94, 96
Cuttlebone, 47

Dangers, list of, 54
Development, 85–87
Diarrhea, 76, 78
Diet:
   additions to basic, 64
   amounts to feed, 61–62
   food preparation, 63–64
   food quality, 59–60
   fruit, vegetables, greens, 62–63
   minerals and trace elements, 65
   people food, 65
   ready-mixed bird-seed, 58–59, 116
   spoiled food, 60–61
   vitamins, 61, 64–65
   water, 64
Distinguishing the sexes, 20–22
Distribution, 12
Dogs, 23–24
Droppings, 71, 76
   changes in, 113
Dull, listless bird, 112–113

Eggs, 13
   binding, 76
   laying, 83–85
Egg tooth, 86
Enclosed birdbath, 49
Enemies, 10
Escapes, 52–53
Eyes, 33

Fat bird, 115–116
Fat reserves, 72
Fatty tumors, 74–75
Fear of touch, 112
Feather mites, 74
Feathers:
   cysts, 75

From a high perch, they have a bird's-eye view!

OF GENERAL IMPORTANCE

excess dropping of, 114
flight, **70**
fluffing up, 93
head, ruffling, 93
healthy, **16**
picking, 117
shaking out, 92–93
Feces, 71
 changes in, 113
Females, 20, 22
Fertilization, 84
Fibrosarcomas, 74
First aid, 73
First free flight, 102–103
Fledgling, **82**
Flight, **9**, **29**, **43**
Flight feathers, **70**
Flock, 9–10, **10–11**, **90–91**
Food. *See* Diet
Food dishes, 47
Food hunt, 106
Formulated diet, 58
Fractures, 103
Fruit, 62–63

Good health, 30–32
Greens, 63, **116**
Grooming, **31**, **71**, 91
Guinea pigs, **106**

Hand rearing, 87
Harmful foods, 65
Harmful plants, 55
Hatchling, 13, **83**, 85–87
Hazards, list of, 54
Head scratching, **83**
Health, signs of, 30, 32
Hearing, 97
Hen, 20
Houseplants, 55
Hygiene:
 bathing, 67–68
 cage cleaning, 70
 feces, 71
 preening, 66–67
 schedule for maintenance, 69

Illness, signs of, 32, 73
Imitating speech, 110
Indoor aviary, 43–44
Infrared light, 73, 78
Injuries, 73–74
Intelligence test, 107
Introducing new cockatiel, 112
Italian millet, 64

Juvenile molt, 87

Ladder game, 106
Landlords, 26
Leg bands, 27, **86**, 87
Legs:
 guarding, 115
 resting on, 90
 stretching, 90
Life expectancy, 12
Long sticks or rods, 64, **64**
Lutino Cockatiel, 34, **37**

Maintenance schedule, 69
Males, 20, 22
Mating, 83

This little fellow isn't quite sure whether to take a bite of basil.

INDEX

Metabolism, 73
Mimicry, 20, 109
Minerals, 65
Mold, 60
Molting, 116–117

Natural branches, 44–47
Naturally-colored Cockatiel, **36–37**
Natural enemies, 10
Nest, 13
Nestling box, 49, 80
Nesting material, 80–81
Nestling period, 12
Nestlings, 13
Nibble sticks, **50**
Nighttime rest, 102
Number of eggs, 12
Nymphicus hollandicus Kerr, 15

Obligate intracellular parasite, 79
Offspring, 10, 12–13
 in the flock, 10–13
Open doors, 54
Outdoor aviary, 44, **49**
Overweight bird, 115–116

Pairs, 22–23, 33, 82–83
Parasites, 74
Pearled (opaline) Cockatiel, **18–19**, **23**, 34, **38–39**
Pelleted commercial feed, 58, 116
People food, 65
Perches, 43–47, **48**
Pets and cockatiels, 23–24
Pet stores, 28
Pied Cockatiel, **17**, 34, **36–38**
Plumage, 14
Poisonous plants, 55
Poisons, 54
Preen gland, 66–67
 obstructed, 75
Preening, 66–67, **67**
Prickly cactus, 55
Psittacosis, 79

Quarrels, 115

Ready-mixed birdseed, 58–59, 116
Red bird mites, 74
Respiratory tract disorders, 79
Rose hips, **46**, **92**
Rot, 60

Safe plants, 55
Scratching, 91–92
Seed diet, 58
Senses, 96–97
Sexing, 20, 22
Sexual maturation, 12
Shock molt, 117
Showers, 68
Sickness, signs of, 32, 73
Sight, 97
Silver Cockatiel, 34
Single bird, 22
Size, 12
Skin changes and injuries, 113–114
Sleeping posture, 90
Small mammals, 24
Smell, 96–97
Snacks, 65
Sneezing, 93, 114
Sour crop, 78
Speech:
 lessons, 109–110
 sounds, 94
Spoiled food, 60–61
Swing, **110**

Tail feathers, 14, **70**
Tail length, 12
Taming, **98–99**, **101**, 101–102
Tassel, making, 105–106
Taste, 97
Toys, 48–49, 108–109
Trace elements, 65
Transport, 79

123

OF GENERAL IMPORTANCE

Treats, 65
Trip home, 98–99
Trust, building, 99–101
Tumors, 74–75

Vacation care, 25
Vegetables, 62–63
Vent, blood on, 113
Vermin, 60–61
Veterinarian, 79
Vitamin therapy, 61
Vitamins, 61, 64–65

Warm weather, 53
Water, 64
  dishes, 47
Way of life, 14
Weight, 12
White-faced Cockatiel, 34, **36, 38–39**
Wild cockatiels:
  appearance, 13–14
  basic information about, 12
  breeding for color, 15–16
  climate, 8–9

flocks, 9–10, **10–11**
natural enemies, 10
offspring, 10, 12–13
Wings:
  flapping, 90
  guarding, 115
  lifting both, 90, **96**
  spreading wide, 90

Yawning, 93, 114
Young cockatiels, 13, 29–30, 33

Rich in vitamins, fruit is an important part of a cockatiel's healthy diet.

USEFUL ADDRESSES AND LITERATURE

Useful Addresses

Organizations

United States
American Cockatiel
 Society, Inc.
9527 60th Lane North
Pinellas Park, FL 33782
http://www.acstiels.com

Association of Avian
 Veterinarians
P.O. Box 811720
Boca Raton, FL 33481-1720
(560) 393-8901
http://www.aav.org/aav.

National Cockatiel
 Society
Membership Secretary
P.O. Box 1363
Avon, CT 06001-1363
e-mail: tiels@sisna.com

American Federation of
 Aviculture
P.O. Box 56218
Phoenix, AZ 85079-6218
(602) 484-0931

International Aviculturists
 Society
P.O. Box 280383
Memphis, TN 38168
(901) 872-7612

Great Britain
The Avicultural Society
The Secretary
Warren Hill,
Halford's Lane
Hartley Wintney,
Hampshire RG27 8AG

The European Aviculture
 Council
c/o Mr. Dave Axtell
P.O. Box 74
Bury St. Edmunds, Suffolk
 IP30 OHS
(This organization has been formed to protect the rights of bird fanciers in Great Britain and Europe.)

Canada
British Columbia
 Avicultural Society
11784-90th Street
North Delta, British
 Columbia V4C 3H6

The Canadian Avicultural
 Society
32 Dronmore Ct.
Willowdale, Ontario M2R
 2H5

Canadian Parrot
 Association
Pine Oaks R. R. #3
St. Catharines, Ontario
 L2R 6P9

Books

Cooke, Dulcie and Freddy Cooke: *Keeping and Breeding Cockatiels*, Blandford Press, London, New York, Sydney, 1987.
Doane, Bonnie Munro: *The Parrot in Health and Illness*, Howell Book House, New York, 1991.
Forshaw, Joseph M.: *Australian Parrots*, 2nd ed., T.F.H. Publications, Inc., Lansdowne, Melbourne, Australia, 1988.
——: *Parrots of the World*, 3rd ed., T.F.H. Publications, Inc., Lansdowne, Melbourne, Australia, 1987.
Lantermann, Werner: *The New Parrot Handbook*, Barron's Educational Series, Inc., Hauppauge, New York, 1987.
Low, Rosemary: *The Complete Book of Parrots*, Barron's Educational Series, Inc., Hauppauge, New York, 1989.
Vriends, Matthew M.: *The New Bird Handbook*, Barron's Educational Series, Inc., Hauppauge, New York, 1989.

OF GENERAL IMPORTANCE

———: *The New Australian Parakeet Handbook*, Barron's Educational Series, Inc., Hauppauge, New York, 1992.

———: *Hand-Feeding and Raising Baby Birds*, Barron's Educational Series, Inc., Hauppauge, New York, 1996.

———: *The Cockatiel Handbook*, Barron's Educational Series, Inc., Hauppauge, New York, 1999.

Magazines
The AFA Watchbird
American Federation of Aviculture
3118 West Thomas Road
Suite 713
Phoenix, AZ 85017

Bird Talk
P.O. Box 57347
Boulder, CO 80323

Birds USA
P.O. Box 55811
Boulder, CO 80322

Cage and Aviary Birds
Prospect House
9–15 Ewell Road
Cheam, Sutton, Surrey
SM3 8B2, England

About the Author
Thomas Haupt, who grew up with animals, has worked since 1992 as a veterinarian in private practice, with a sizeable number of birds in his care. He keeps many birds himself, particularly cockatiels, budgerigars, and parrots. He also maintains a clinic for injured wild animals.

About the Photographer
The photographs in this book were taken by Karin Skogstad, except for those by: Juniors/Liebold: page 20; Juniors/Wegner: pages 27, 38 bottom left, 48, 67, 82 right; Kuhn: pages 98, 99, 104, 106, 115, 121, 128 top left; Pfeffer: pages 36 bottom center, bottom right, 37 top left, top right, bottom right, 39 top left, bottom left, 49; Reinhard: pages 8, 9, 18–19, 29, 31, 34–35, 36 top left, 37 bottom right, 39 top right; Schweiger/Arendt: Pages 6–7, 10–11, 90–91.

Karin Skogstad has worked as a freelance journalist and photographer since 1979. She specializes in animals and plants.

About the Artist
Renate Holzner works as a freelance illustrator in Regensburg, Germany. Her broad repertoire ranges from line drawings to photorealistic illustrations and computer graphics.

Photographs on Cover and Full-Page Spreads:
Front cover: Cock with natural markings (large and small photos).
Pages 2–3: Fresh greenery adds welcome variety to the menu and is good for the birds' health as well.
Pages 6–7: Cockatiels cavort in their natural habitat.
Pages 40–41: The cockatiel investigates with beak and tongue to determine what's good to eat.
Pages 89–90: Italian millet ranks high on the list of popular snacks.
Back cover: A pied male and a lutino share a millet spray.

IMPORTANT NOTE

Important Note

No one who is allergic to feathers or feather dust should keep birds. If you have any doubts, consult your physician before you buy a bird.

Chlamydiosis, psittacosis, or parrot fever, called ornithosis in other birds, is an OIP infection that can be contracted by humans if they inhale dust from the feces of infected birds or have contact with their nasal secretions (see page 79). If you suspect infection, take the cockatiel to the veterinarian. If you have cold or flu symptoms, by all means consult your physician, who should also be informed that you keep birds.

English-language version © Copyright 2000 by
Barron's Educational Series, Inc.
© 1999 by Gräfe und Unzer Verlag GmbH, München.
Published originally under the title *Der Nymphensittich*.
English translation by Celia Bohannon.
Consulting Editor: April Romagnano, Ph.D., DVM,
Dipl. ABVP (Avian Practice)

All rights reserved.
No part of this book may be reproduced in any form, by photostat, microfilm, xerography, or any other means, or incorporated into any information retrieval system, electronic or mechanical, without the written permission of the copyright owner.

All inquiries should be addressed to:
Barron's Educational Series, Inc.
250 Wireless Boulevard
Hauppauge, New York 11788
http://www.barronseduc.com

International Standard Book
No. 0-7641-5230-0

*Library of Congress Catalog
Card No. 00-101229*

Printed in Hong Kong

9 8 7 6 5 4 3 2 1

Who's the handsome fellow in the mirror? Let's take a closer look!